More
Costumes
for the
Stage

Sheila Jackson

More
Costumes
for the
Stage

The Herbert Press

First published in Great Britain 1993
Reprinted 1998
by the Herbert Press, an imprint of
A & C Black (Publishers) Limited
35 Bedford Row, London WC1R 4JH
ISBN 1-871569-54-0

House editor: Brenda Herbert
Designed by Pauline Harrison

A CIP catalogue record for this book is available from
the British Library.

Set in Linotype Cartier
Typeset by Nene Phototypesetters Ltd, Northampton

Printed in the United States of America

Contents

Introduction

This book is intended as a guide and source of ideas for people working in the amateur theatre or in fringe areas or schools where economy and the simplest methods are all-important. My previous book, *Costumes for the Stage*, covered a wide field of simple instruction and ideas, and I hope that the present one will fill in any gaps and spark off some new creativity as well as providing enough basic information for those who have not read the earlier one. Some overlap is inevitable, but I have tried to vary the sources I have used and, with the exception of the page on mask-making, the illustrations are new and will give an alternative approach to any area previously covered.

The book's real purpose is to draw the attention of those who enjoy working in the theatre, but have no formal training, to a wider vision of design and creativity than they may yet have encountered, and to encourage them to aim higher when thinking about design and be more adventurous and inventive in all its aspects. I have included additional guidance in some more specialized areas such as dance and music, and I have introduced the subject of ethnic costume which was not included before; but the field of costume is so broad that it is possible to give only a taste of all the goodies waiting to be discovered by the keen researcher, and I hope that people who use this book will be fired by my suggestions to discover much more for themselves.

There has been a great increase recently in the volume of easily available research material. Not so many years ago, designers had to rely on a few books and costume sources and a few badly lit and inadequately displayed costumes in one or two musuems. Today it is a different story: the range of material in libraries, musuems and art galleries is wider and includes information about the dress of ordinary people and not only of those in the forefront of fashion.

Enquiry should also extend beyond the world of historical clothes; those with lively minds will want to look at and make use of all kinds of sources which at first seem unrelated – a visit to the zoo, a pottery exhibition, a walk along a foreign street or souk – even the packaging in a supermarket. Pick up a buckle, a handful of shells, a length of braid, and suddenly you have a costume in your hand. The theatre is a magic world and there is magic all around you; all you have to do is to train your eye to see it and make the magic yourself!

1 The work place

For nearly all drama productions, the creation and realization of the costumes involves a considerable amount of work. It is therefore sensible to give some thought to how and where this is to be done. In an ideal situation, it will be in a large, light workroom conveniently equipped with all the tools of the trade; but in reality most people working in costume, whether amateur or professional, find themselves settling for more modest amenities. Careful thought, before you start, about the equipment and space you will need for producing good results will save frustration and disappointment later and will help you to budget effectively for essentials.

One essential requirement for the workspace is good ventilation, because certain materials such as glues and spray paints give off toxic fumes.

Minimum equipment must include a firm table large enough for cutting out on, a sewing machine capable of stitching various weights of material, one or two dress stands, an iron, an ironing board and a sleeve board.

A padded arm that can be attached to a dress stand is useful for fitting sleeves; see diagram (a) on page 9. Cut two pieces of calico as shown, to the required size, and stitch them together round the edge, leaving a gap to insert padding. Fill the shaded area with kapok padding, stitch across p–q to hold it in place, and then stitch round the top. The arm can be pinned to the stand when required.

Another firmly padded shape such as (d) is useful when pressing awkward corners of a garment.

All equipment must be in a good light. One or more Anglepoise lamps are useful for directing light onto specific areas.

An electric or gas ring, and a kettle that can be used for steaming operations – to remodel hats or renovate fabrics such as velvet, etc. which have been crushed – should be available.

Shelves or cupboards for storage are essential. These can accommodate fabrics, containers for small items such as pins and fastenings, and boxes for elastic, tape and other haberdashery. Look out for containers – cardboard, polystyrene or the excellent plastic boxes in bright colours that are thrown away in street markets. Strong plastic mesh onion sacks from the same source are also good for stowing shoes, scraps of fabric and trimming, ends of quilted fabric for padding, or cleaning rags. Cotton reels can be stored in a large glass jar or hung on nails or pieces of dowel fixed to a strip of wood (page 9, e).

For storing costumes a rail must be provided, with a supply of coat- and skirt-hangers. Wire coat-hangers from dry cleaners will need cardboard or padded fabric covers to prevent the wire shape from spoiling the shoulder-line of garments; see diagram and pattern on page 9 (c). Cut the card or wadding as indicated and, after cutting the slits x–y, overlap the cut edges, moving point x to x¹, and staple together. The distance between these two points is variable and the angle of the shoulders can thus be varied. A layer of papier mâché over the shape will give extra substance. Really heavy costumes need strong wooden hangers (f). Plastic hangers, unless of good quality, will bend or break easily. Costumes hung on a rail should be covered with a clean cloth or old sheet to keep them free from dust. Do not use polythene bags or sheeting as this will attract the dirt.

A large rubbish bin (or box) and a dustpan and brush will keep the workroom tidy. Keep plenty of newspaper and rags or disposable cleaning cloths handy. Make it a rule that no-one should eat or drink in the workroom – spills and sticky messes can spoil careful work.

It is advisable, if possible, to divide the workroom into two areas – one for cutting, fitting and sewing and the other for messy work such as dyeing, painting and printing and any work that involves adhesives. If this is not feasible, try to arrange a painting week or weekend when the room can be cleared for activity without fear of dye or paint finding its way on to garments for which it was not intended and completed work can be hung or spread out to dry. Paints, dyes and adhesives should be kept separately from sewing materials. A rack will be needed to store basic tools such as pliers, screwdrivers, hammers, a small hack saw and a drill. Save boxes for screws, nails, rolls of wire, twine and thread. Hang squeegees and brushes from hooks, to keep the blades and bristles in good condition. Label everything in the workroom clearly and keep a modest first aid kit in an accessible place.

A pin-board just inside the door will provide easy reference to notices and can display a work chart which records deadlines, fitting times, meetings, job allotments, vital addresses and telephone numbers.

Measurements of performers can either be kept in a looseleaf measurement book or on index cards in a filing box. The most important measurements are:

height	hips	waist to ground
chest	nape to waist	collar size
waist	outer arm bent	head circumference
across back	inside leg from crutch to floor	shoe size

It is a help to photocopy a supply of sheets or cards that can be filled in as measurements are taken so that essentials will not be overlooked. For some costumes specific measurements may be necessary. Keep all measurements firmly in the file or card index, because to mislay them can be disastrous; and retain them after the production unless an actor is definitely not to be used again. Addresses and telephone numbers should be on the cards; and cards need to be updated from time to time as people's statistics fluctuate. It is advisable to take measurements personally if possible, as actors are not always totally honest in this respect!

Use a good tape measure – old ones stretch and are inaccurate. Tapes are often marked with metric measurements on one side and imperial on the other, so be sure to read the right side! A yardstick is the best tool to use for measuring skirt lengths from the floor and is also useful for drawing long straight lines when making patterns.

When facilities are very limited, use can be made of willing outworkers who will take over the making of one or more costumes. It is wise for a competent cutter to cut out the costumes and pin them as far as possible before passing them on to others for sewing, and it is essential to supply clear instructions for making up. If possible arrange a meeting or get-together to discuss methods and procedures for sewing and fitting and the differences between theatrical work and home dressmaking, and to answer any questions that may arise. Painting and printing can be done before making up and it is unwise to leave this part of the work to be done individually – good needlewomen are not always good with a paintbrush. Also, the sense of style will be lost if too many helpers have a finger in the pie! Call in all the finished garments in good time to check that they are satisfactory and contribute to the special look of the production and to apply any extra decoration that is necessary. Remember to thank people for their hard work.

In the Workroom.

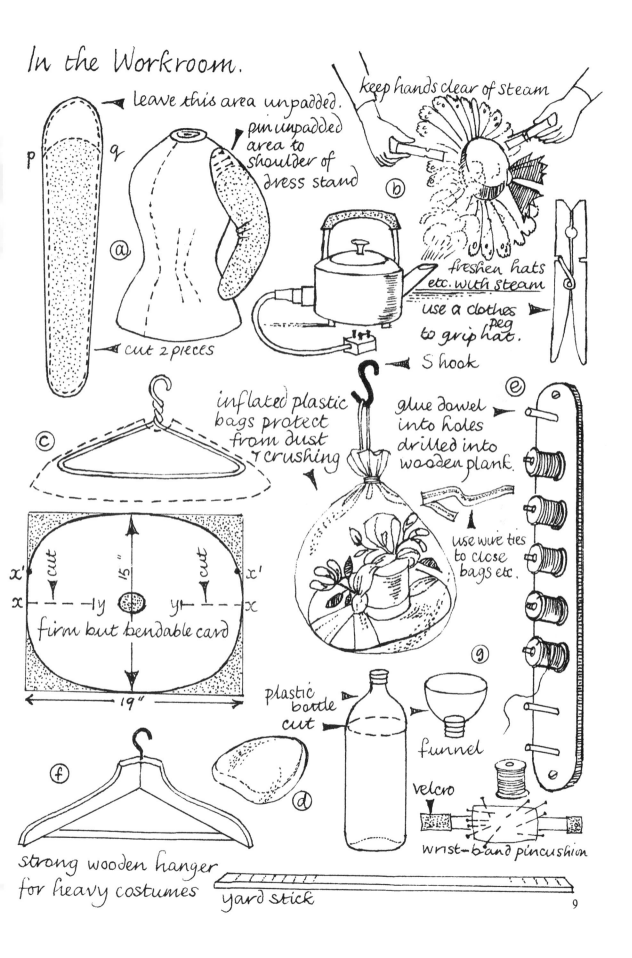

leave this area unpadded.

pin unpadded area to shoulder of dress stand

p   q

ⓐ

cut 2 pieces

keep hands clear of steam

ⓑ

freshen hats etc. with steam

use a clothes peg to grip hat.

S hook

inflated plastic bags protect from dust + crushing

glue dowel into holes drilled into wooden plank.

ⓔ

use wire ties to close bags etc.

ⓒ

cut   cut

x'   x'
x   y   y   x

15"

firm but bendable card

19"

plastic bottle cut

funnel

velcro

wrist-band pincushion

ⓖ

ⓕ

ⓓ

strong wooden hanger for heavy costumes

yard stick

9

2 Considering the budget

The cost of producing costumes today, whether for the professional or amateur stage, can be prohibitive. All fabrics and haberdashery are now becoming much more expensive; elastics, fastenings, braids are no longer minor items, even the cost of sewing thread adds greatly to the final bill. So it is important to make sure that these necessities are included in the costing. This means that the designer on a low budget must be inventive and resourceful from the start, planning carefully and making use of all kinds of surplus materials. This need not necessarily be inhibiting – very good designs can be achieved by making a virtue of restrictions and overcoming them with imagination and flair.

Make a collection of all available unwanted items – old sheets, blankets, towels, tights, all kinds of T-shirts. Other people's rejects such as bubble wrap, corrugated cardboard, plastic articles, pieces of polystyrene will all have their uses when building up headdresses, masks and costume props. Old knitted garments should be unravelled; the wool, rehanked and washed, is reusable for knitting medieval hoods, caps, bonnets, etc. Items which can be cannibalized can be picked up cheaply from charity shops and jumble sales. Training the eye to spot possibilities is very important – the vital factor is not what it is but what it can be made into.

When purchasing new materials, *think first*. This will save a great many mistakes and much wastage. Purchase wisely and economically by tracking down inexpensive sources of fabrics in street markets and stalls or shops selling off-cuts and ends of ranges. During the seasonal sales, look for remnants of cloth and trimmings in both the fabric and furnishing departments of large stores. Unbleached calico is still fairly inexpensive and as it takes dye and paint well and can also be very attractive in its natural state it is a worthwhile purchase. It has the added advantage of being available in a variety of widths. For a stiffer fabric, hessian can also be painted or stencilled successfully. Butter muslin (or mull) is cheap but soon loses its crispness and begins to look depressed after a few wearings.

When the patterns have been made, work out carefully the amount of fabric you will need and, if the budget allows, buy an extra half metre; this is usually an investment as it can be used for alterations or patching when the costume comes into use a second time. Do not be deterred by the restraints of a low budget. Instead, let it be a challenge – avoid wrongly-directed ambition and extravagance and err on the side of simplicity.

Using *objets trouvés*

In addition to the items mentioned above, all kind of *objets trouvés* will be useful in putting a show together. Look out for them at all times, not only when under pressure of an impending production. Never pass a skip or dumper truck without eyeing it for some useful piece of junk.

Here are some ideas:
For *armour* bottle tops, papier mâché fruit trays, egg boxes, plastic bubble wrap
For *decoration on belts, crowns and heavy jewelry* corks, plastic screw caps, plastic and tin lids, odds and ends of string and rope, drinking straws

For wigs soft plastic mesh, metal foil strip, beads, horsehair from old sofas, garden raffia, twine (see page 000)

For making papier mâché newspaper and tissue paper, bandages

For masks large jiffy bags or strong brown paper bags

For jewelry beads, buttons, odd earrings, dried seeds

For children's costumes paper sacks

For hats, headdresses, posies, garlands feathers, dried grasses and flowers, artificial leaves and flowers

For decoration generally natural objects such as fir cones, shells, seeds and pebbles can be glued to many artifacts.

Suggestions for the use of many of these will be found in the later chapters of the book and several of the drawings illustrate how they can be employed for specific purposes.

Other found objects have uses in the workroom – yoghourt pots for mixing and holding paint (beware of some paints that dissolve plastic!); small plastic or polystyrene trays from frozen foods for holding beads and sequins spread out for selection; screw-top glass jars to hold paint and also for storing buttons, screws etc.; unwanted saucers and plates on which to mix powder colours and watercolours. Excellent funnels can be made from plastic bottles (see diagram on page 9). Nylon tights are good for straining paint which has become lumpy in storage.

There is, in fact, no end to the uses of other people's detritus!

3 Historical costume

This chapter deals with the development of historical European costume. The importance of the evolution of clothes and its bearing on dress in the theatre cannot be over-stressed; it is the source to which all designers must constantly return and its influence on action and life style is full of interest. For the costume designer it should be an inspiration rather than an end in itself. The responsibility of the historian and museum curator is to investigate, present and record the original article, the job of the designer is to select the relevant aspect of the period and distil it. It may therefore be necessary to dig deeper into reference works to supplement the information given here, which is of necessity only an outline.

The applications for period costume that I have illustrated are not intended as designs to be followed precisely; they show one way of using reference sources for a particular production and aim to demonstrate the influence of character on costume, how one period links with another, and how, quite often, specific types of character are common to all periods. The drawings are meant to complement the text with further suggestions towards how historical costume can be adapted to simple creation, presentation and a stylistic approach. Although I have related the drawings to a specific play, they should serve just as well as starting points for other productions of a similar type and period.

This section of the book should not be considered in isolation. It is intended for use in conjunction with the ideas and information set out in the rest of the book. Further headdresses, details and accessory diagrams and patterns in other chapters will be helpful in filling in what may, at first, appear to be gaps.

There are simple patterns, drawn to the scale of one square: 50mm (2 ins), and diagrams which are in proportion but to no particular scale. These patterns are intended as a guide: it will be necessary to adapt and redraft them to an individual set of measurements, with adjustments for an exaggerated figure or for any padding that may be required. Leave ample seam allowances when cutting out, so that garments can be adjusted at fittings, and do not trim the final seams too closely if the garment will eventually go into stock and may need alteration at a later date.

Patterns can be made on squared drafting paper (obtainable at a draper's suppliers), brown paper or newspaper; those that are to serve as a basis for cutting further patterns should be transferred to calico with a wax pencil, including balance marks which will guarantee that the edges come together at correct points when making up. Always pin and baste carefully; in some cases machining a seam with a long loose stitch will make tricky fitting more exact – but it must be a stitch that can be easily ripped out for alteration. Care in preparing a garment for fitting is time well spent – but do not take the work too far before fitting, as this may mean extensive and difficult alteration.

THE SHAPE AND DEVELOPMENT OF HISTORICAL COSTUME

The importance of good shapes in stage costume cannot be over-emphasized. Strong clear lines are the result of good, confident cutting – understanding the cut of a garment, with proper attention paid to the grain of the cloth, is essential. Studying the development of historical costume helps to train the eye to appreciate the qualities of line, shape and proportion; and, because dress always reflects the social history of the time, it is also a good guide to the manners and behaviour portrayed in the plays and literature of the period.

Paintings and prints should be studied not only for their costume information but also for the light they cast on posture, which is a very important factor in presenting dress. An excellent costume will disappoint if it is worn in a slovenly or incorrect manner. Shoes are also an important factor in correct movement and posture: the height and shape of heels (if any) and the length of the toes both influence the way in which the wearer stands and walks.

It is not possible to show in the drawings that accompany this section a complete panorama of the progression of style through the centuries. I have chosen examples that are most typical of their time and likely to be useful for most purposes. There are now very many costume books available, and art gallery shops have useful postcards, but there is no substitute for looking at the real thing and a visit to a costume museum or a picture gallery is the best source of information. Bear in mind, however, that the display of costumes on lay figures may not always show off shape and stance to the best advantage.

Being in vogue has always been important to both men and women who aim to achieve the face and figure most admired in their time, and their dress is designed to draw attention to and enhance the attributes fashionably considered desirable. The medieval Venus had small high breasts and a large belly; subsequently, other features such as soft shoulders and dimpled arms, tiny waists, voluptuous bosoms, the mature matronly figure of Edwardian womanhood or the boyish figure of the twenties girl were all considered high fashion in their day.

The main points of fashionable style and shape and their development through six centuries are set out below and illustrated on pages 14–19. Further examples and details for all periods, with suggestions for their application, will be found on pages 21–74.

Medieval to sixteenth century

Women

The medieval gown falls from narrow shoulders to a wide hemline which always touches the floor, often trailing behind. The drawing on page 14 (a) shows a fourteenth-century cotehardie worn over a waistless dress with tight sleeves. A wimple, which could be variously arranged, covers the hair.

In the fifteenth century the bust is still small but a belt encircles the high waist. A centre-front seam allows extra fullness for cartridge pleats over the belly, which on occasion are padded for extra emphasis. Sleeves have widened to a trumpet shape. The headdress is a truncated hennen – a style introduced from the Middle East by the crusaders. Hair is still concealed; the fashionably high forehead may be shaved. Flat shoes have pointed toes.

By the early sixteenth century the shape has become square. The heavy dress, worn over a padded roll to support the skirt, has a waist seam and the sleeves are turned back to show linen under-sleeves. Hair sometimes shows at the front of the headdress, which may be gable-shaped. Shoes (for both women and men) are bun-toed.

The Elizabethan woman's figure (page 15, a) is disguised by the stiff and artificial

cotehardie

head frails

surcoat

C14

ⓐ

C15

ⓑ

kidney shaped hip pads

padded cartridge pleats

Early C16

ⓒ

Skirt may be split to show petti'coat

bun toed shoe

long toed shoe - poulaine

hood with liripipe

ⓓ

magyar sleeves

houppelande

chaperon

bag hat

ⓔ

dagged edging

thonging

C14

short boot.

C15

bun toed shoes

Early C16

ⓕ

14

ⓐ
1600

over skirt can be split to show the petticoat

1629
ⓑ

scooped line at skirt waist creates spoon folds

muffs are worn

ⓒ

White muslin cap under hat

lawn undersleeves

1640

puritans 1650

ruff patterns 1600

ⓓ

stockings rolled over knees

collar mounted on too deep band

lace collar & cuffs

ⓔ

ⓕ

straight hair

small buckles

puritans wear dark colours

15

(a) 1690 fontange

(b) 1750 straw hat lace cap

(c) 1790

(d) 1678 fur muff

(e) 1740

(f) 1790 frac coat fobs bicorn hat

16

shape of her attire. The bodice has narrowed to a point, emphasized by the cartwheel skirt. A ruff or decorative collar frames the face.

Men

In the fourteenth century, the magyar-sleeved tunic is worn by rich and poor alike, in various lengths, the difference in status shown by the quality of cloth and decoration. Tights or loose trousers (see pattern, page 85, *f*) cover the legs, often tied below the knee with thongs (page 14, *d*).

In the fifteenth century the robe worn by well-to-do men has set-in sleeves, often loose and decoratively dagged (scalloped) (page 14, *e*); the fabric is pulled into pleats centre front and back which are held in place by a belt. Big hats, chaperons and hoods with a long liripipe bound into a turban shape are all worn.

The early sixteenth-century man's outline is very square (page 14, *f*), matching the squat doorways of Tudor architecture. He wears a sleeveless coat over a knee-length pleated tunic with a waist seam. Fabrics are heavy – often brocade or embroidery.

The Elizabethan man, slimmer and more elegant though much puffed and padded, cuts a dashing figure (page 15, *d*). This is set off by short trunk hose or canions (a kind of breeches) which draw attention to the length of leg. Slashing on sleeves reveals rich fabrics underneath.

Seventeenth century

Women

By 1640 a softer, more flowing line emerges, showing much more flesh (page 15, *b*). The waist is quite high and the basque is all that remains of the cartwheel waist of the Elizabethans. Soft shiny silks and satins, lace and pearls add to the air of sumptuousness.

This development is halted during the mid-century period of the Commonwealth in England. The basic shape is similar but dark stuffs such as wool and linen replace luxurious silks. Prim collars, cuffs and aprons emphasize the Puritan worthiness (*c*).

This rigidity is replaced in the Restoration period after 1660 by a swing to the opposite extreme, bringing a style of great artificiality that will continue to evolve and develop over the next hundred years. The woman's dress becomes puffed, beribboned and fringed, the shape vertical (page 16, *a*). On her head she wears the fontange (a lace cap with an upstanding pleated front and lace streamers).

Men

The flamboyant figure of 1640 (page 15, *e*) has flowing locks, his hat is feathered and his knees beribboned. Lace is much favoured. Then, similarly to his female companion, the Puritan (*f*) is dressed severely in dark heavy stuffs only relieved by linen collar and cuffs. Bucket boots emphasize his earthy character.

In the second half of the century, feathers in hats and curled and flowing locks return, with large muffs, large cuffs, large hats and flamboyant gloves and stocks (page 16, *d*).

Eighteenth century

Women

Continuing the late-seventeenth-century development, by the middle of the eighteenth century the skirt has extended sideways, supported by 'improvers' or panniers of

(a) 1814 ball dress

kid gloves

(b) 1843 bodice

padded rouleaux

(c) 1862

bustle pad

(d) 1885 walking dress

(e) 1807

boot 1807

straw hat 1807

(f) cravat

1865

(g) 1885

18

1905

leg of mutton
sleeve

cloche
hat

1926

1946

1965

ⓐ

ⓑ

ⓒ

ⓓ

1907

1926

1946

1965

ⓦ

ⓔ

ⓕ

ⓖ

19

whalebone and wire (page 16, *b*). There is a more pastoral look – the breath of a shepherdess (albeit a rather artificial one) – about the grand lady who steps lightly in her sprigged chintz or silk.

Towards the end of the century there is a further trend towards informality (*c*) – a small bustle pad supports the skirt at the back in place of the wide panniers; soft, gauzy fichus envelope the shoulders, a sash or ribbon may encircle the waist. Shawls, stoles and muffs are carried. Hair puffed up and frizzed with side ringlets enlarges the head shape and this is sometimes covered by a large muslin cap or bonnet known as a caléche.

Men

The mid-eighteenth-century male figure, still exaggerated but more trim, wears a wide-skirted coat over a fine waistcoat (page 16, *e*). Silk stockings are rolled over the breeches at the knee. Note the tricorne hat, a round hat with the brim rolled to produce a three-cornered shape.

At the end of the century the dandified figure (*f*) takes the stage in his waspish waistcoat and immensely high collar and stock. Narrow, tight sleeves help the exaggerated narrowness of the figure.

Nineteenth century

Women

At the turn of the century, the casting off of all foundation garments is a surprising development, allowing the natural figure to be revealed. At its most extreme, the fashion is for flimsy, often transparent, fabrics that hardly conceal the body. Dainty soft slippers encase the feet and long soft kid gloves the arms (page 18, *a*).

Twenty years or so of this abandon is followed by a return to inhibiting tight lacing in the middle and late nineteenth century (page 18, *b* and *c*). Voluminous, concealing skirts are worn over many petticoats and a crinoline cage – a structured shape designed for a caged domestic life. From the 1860s onwards, skirts gradually become narrower with the emphasis at the back, supported by the bustle, a frame of wire and horsehair, or more simply a pad worn over the behind – a new area of fashion interest! The constricting bodice is constructed with many seams and worn over a complicated corset. Hats and bonnets are small.

Men

The Regency Rake is another dandy whose garments are similar to his predecessor's but are worn more casually. His cutaway coat has a fashionable velvet collar and brass buttons, and he carries a bicorne hat. He may wear buckled shoes or tasselled boots (page 18, *e*).

Well-dressed but worthy, the mid-Victorian gentleman wears a morning coat (*f*). Although breeches are still worn, narrow-legged trousers reaching to the ankle are making their appearance for the first time, and will continue. Tailoring now becomes important and remains so until after World War II. Neckwear is less flamboyant, stocks being replaced by cravats and ties. Top hats are much worn. Elastic-sided boots for formal wear and lace-up boots for the working man replace buckled shoes or high boots. Later (*g*) a variety of suits become generally popular, made in suitings and tweeds, and coloured waistcoats (vests) are sometimes worn. The drawing shows a bowler hat.

Twentieth century

Women

Edwardian dresses may be frothy and lacy or very trim (page 19, *a*) with shoulder emphasis – either large puffed sleeves or the fashionable leg-o'-mutton shape. A boned cummerbund draws attention to a small waist.

Following World War I and the emancipation of women, the boyish 'flapper' image appears. Legs are exposed for the first time ever – a new erotic area to excite notice. Evening dresses such as (*b*) fit in with the jazz age and the new freedom in clothes coincides with an enthusiasm for sport. After World War II and wartime austerity, a longing for attractive, glamorous clothes results in Dior's 'New Look' with nipped-in waist and longer skirt of greatly increased yardage (*c*). With this goes an elegant small head – but by the 1970s the 'beehive' hairdo surmounts neat, mix-and-match outfits and jersey is a popular fabric (*d*).

Men

For the Edwardians, a morning coat worn with a double-breasted waistcoat, a cravat and a top hat is correct formal wear (page 19, *e*). The coat, shown here with silk facings, is almost always black.

The three-buttoned suit of the mid twenties is worn with only the middle button of the jacket fastened (*f*). Trousers have turn-ups, are worn shorter, and are frequently of grey flannel. The trilby hat in soft felt can be worn with the brim up or down.

Immediately after World War II men's clothes are fairly easy to wear and conventional in cut. Sports jackets (*g*) are worn by young and old alike, usually with grey flannels or with Bedford cord trousers, shoes are still laced and suede is looked on as not quite nice! Hats have become rare except for formal events. By 1965 there is a great change in the whole attitude to clothes, with young people finding a new freedom. The final drawing (*h*) shows a collarless jacket as affected by the Beatles in their early days; the collar stands higher on the neck but a regulation tie is still part of the outfit. Slip-on shoes have cuban heels.

ANCIENT EGYPTIAN COSTUME

From the representation in wall paintings, the Old Kingdom Egyptians appear to have worn a loincloth (page 22, *b*) wrapped several times round the body and girded. As the dynasties became more sophisticated and opulent, the garment worn by the nobles was of more costly and decorative material and more cunningly draped, thus distinguishing them from the lower classes. From 1000 BC, New Kingdom Egyptians of both sexes wore the kalasiris, a one-piece garment taking several different forms. It may finish above or below the chest, held in place by a diagonal shoulder strap (page 23, *a*) – or reach the neck, and have either long or short sleeves (see pattern on page 23 which can be adapted as required). The kalasiris worn by women always reaches the ankles. Rectangular, round or oval cloaks are either chest-length (page 22, *b*) or elbow-length (page 22, *c*) and pleated at the front. Many of the garments represented in the paintings are so skin-tight that it is difficult to understand how their wearers ever moved (page 22, *e*) – it is thought some knitted fabric must have been used, so that for theatrical use today it is feasible to use jerseys and knitted fabrics that will stretch easily. Very fine and transparent materials are

Egyptians

ⓐ ⓑ ⓒ

ⓖ

1350 BC

ⓕ

heavy wig
Knitting.
is a possibility.

n.b.
hand.
pleating
See chapter
Fabrics plain
+ patterned.

ⓗ

ⓓ

ⓔ

painted
or
decorated
bead collar

stencilled
pattern

transparent
skirt

Application of Egyptian Costume.

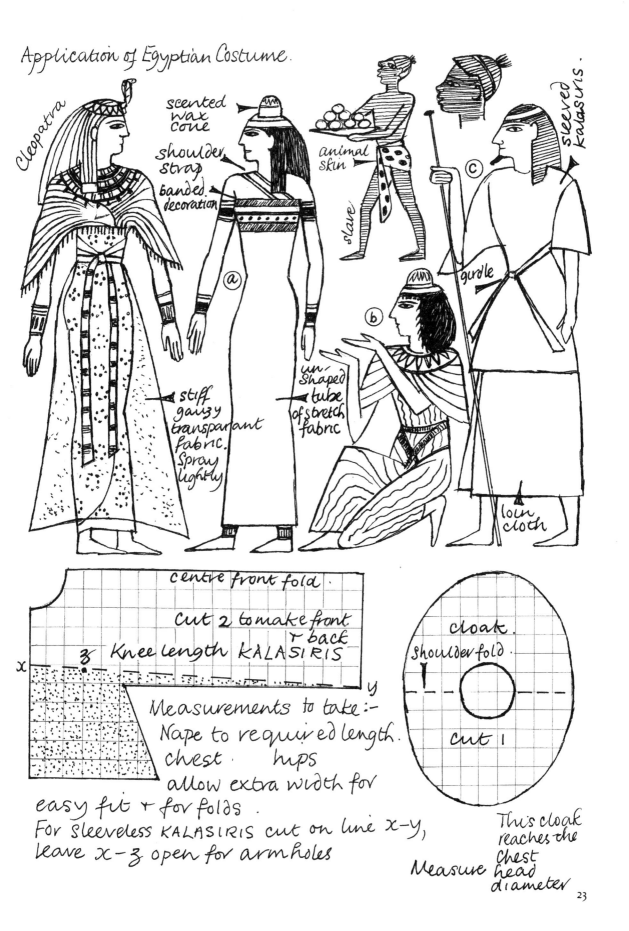

Cleopatra

scented wax cone

shoulder strap

banded decoration

animal skin

slave

sleeved kalasiris.

ⓒ

girdle

ⓐ

ⓑ

stiff gauzy transparent fabric. Spray lightly

un-shaped tube of stretch fabric

loin cloth

centre front fold.

cut 2 to make front + back Knee length KALASIRIS

x

3

y

Measurements to take :-
Nape to required length.
chest   hips
        allow extra width for
easy fit + for folds.
For sleeveless KALASIRIS cut on line x-y,
leave x-3 open for arm holes

cloak.
shoulder fold.

cut 1

This cloak reaches the chest
Measure head diameter

23

frequently depicted for the nobles, and draping and pleating are important features (page 22, *c* and *h*).

Wall paintings in tombs and temples provide marvellous costume reference, and reproductions are easily available. The richness of both pattern and colour give ample opportunity for the use of painting and stencilling when creating costumes.

Application
Shakespeare's *Antony and Cleopatra* is an interesting play to design for, requiring a contrast between the costumes of the conquering Romans (see page 27) and those of the very ancient Nile valley civilization in decline.

Cleopatra's dress (page 23) should be rich and seductive and the tightly stretched undergarment would look well in a shiny gold stretch fabric, lightly patterned so that the stretch will not distort the pattern. A light spray of bronze or silver-gold will help to maintain the stiffness of the gauzy over-garment. A pleated, bead-fringed cloak is worn around the shoulders, and beading and embroidery decorate the girdle and collar.

On the same page, *a* and *b* show two ladies of the Egyptian court – the standing figure wears a tube of stretch fabric with a decorative band across the chest, the other a draped or pleated kalasiris, a draped shoulder cape and a decorative collar necklace. Both their headdresses include the scented wax cone which gradually melted, giving off a seductive scent. The Soothsayer (*c*) wears the sleeved kalasiris over a long loincloth; conversely a draped loincloth was sometimes worn over a long kalasiris.

Wigs need to be large enough and must look formal rather than realistic. They can be based on a net cap which has been lightly padded, to which silk, wool, cotton or wire wool can be attached – the padding will reduce the amount of covering material required. Details of the Cleopatra headdress are given in the chapter on headgear, page 104(*c*).

ANCIENT GREEK COSTUME

The basis of all ancient Greek dress, both male and female, is a rectangle of cloth. All forms of the costume can in theory be produced without the use of scissors, needles or thread, but this may not always be appropriate for a theatrical production, because the performer needs to feel secure and comfortable in his costume and will not be accustomed to controlling loose drapery.

Various low-budget fabrics are suitable and should be carefully chosen for their weight and draping qualities. Wools and crepes, old sheets or towelling will be best for cloaks, tunics and robes, but for crinkled and pulled pleating (see page 93) it is essential to use lightweight materials such as butter muslin, cheesecloth, thin silk, lawn or fabrics which do not have too much spring in them. Remember that for pleated garments it is necessary to increase the width of the material – experiment with a width of the fabric to see how it responds to pleating.

Garments include the chiton, worn by men and women, a tunic of various length worn over the naked body; it is frequently coloured and adorned with a showy fastening. Worn by women only is the peplos or over-dress. Both these garments may have a girdle, or cords or braid may be used to control pleats and folds. The chlamys is a small cloak usually brooched; the hymation is an ampler mantle worn by elderly men and by women, less often brooched. Thonged sandals or soft knee-length boots are the usual footwear. The latter can be made from thick knee-length socks. The rope soles of discarded espadrilles with leather thonging or webbing threaded through them will make very convincing sandals. First cut away the toe part and then arrange the thonging as shown (page 26, *c*).

Ionian costume, worn by the Greeks until after the Persian Wars in the fifth century BC, was brightly coloured and richly decorated (page 27, *a*, *b* and *e*). This can be represented by stencilling, painting and printing (see chapter 8). A good decorative border is shown in the drawing (*c*) on page 26.

Young men never wear hats unless they are travellers (page 26, *e* and *h*), but hats are usually worn by old men, slaves (*f*) and soldiers.

Actors in Greek tragedy wore costumes based on priestly robes, for whatever the story the dramas were religious in intention, but the colour of the garments had great significance and where appropriate robes would appear torn, in grief or anger. Conversely, actors in the comedies were dressed like common people – short chitons were of shoddy material and the actors were frequently padded, both on the stomach and the posterior, using a vest-like garment to hold the padding in place.

Application

I have chosen Shakespeare's A *Midsummer Night's Dream*, which is set in Athens, to illustrate an application of Greek costume (page 28). Usefully, it encompasses characters from various strata of society.

The nobles, Theseus and Hippolyta, are richly decorated. He wears a pleated tunic girt at the waist – the narrow pleating will require a lightweight fabric, whereas the long cloak needs a heavier cloth. His laurel garland signifies that he is high-born. Hippolyta, being an Amazon queen, might at some time have a leopard skin draped across her hymation instead of the decorated peplos of the drawing. Jewelry and an important coronet proclaim her nobility. Helena and Demetrius are well-born Athenians – his chiton is decorated and the cloak he wears will be useful to wrap round his lover when they sleep in the wood. Over a long chiton she wears a peplos which is bound across and under her breasts to keep the many folds in place.

Barefooted Puck wears a goatskin – frequently used in Greek drama – over a loincloth. Bottom provides a good opportunity to employ the padding mentioned above for characters in comedy, and this will suit his swaggering personality. A theatrical, jokey helmet suitable for Pyramus is shown (*a*). All the 'mechanicals' will wear short chitons similar to that on page 26 (*g*) showing a butcher and (*f*) another worker who wears a loincloth and a cap. A more roughly made version of (*d*) on this page would be useful for the 'mechanical' who acts the part of the lion.

Ancient Greeks

a
b
g
h
d
f
e
HERCULES
ARKESILAS KING OF CYRENE
sandal from espadrille

26

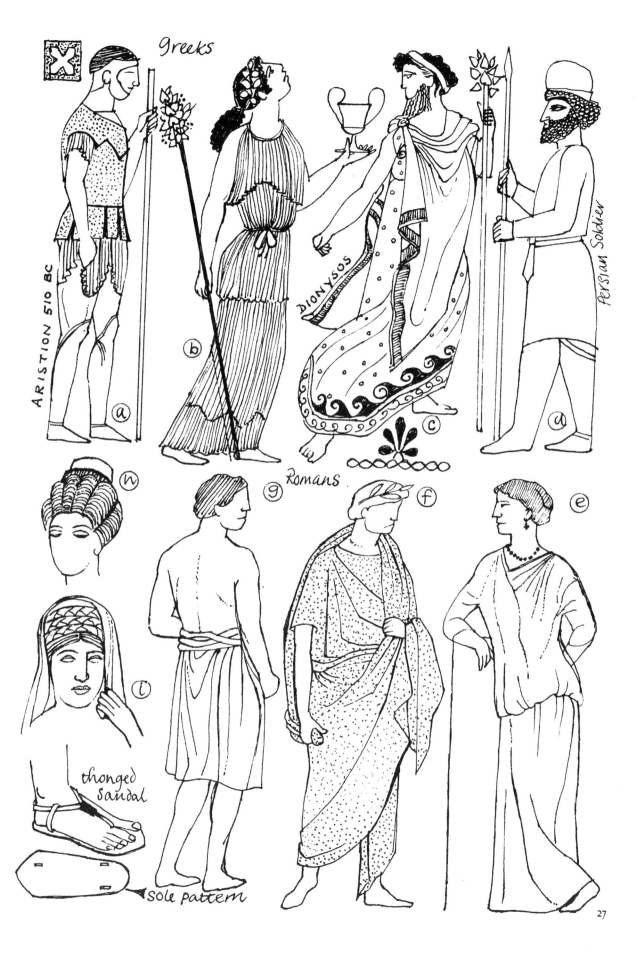

greeks

ARISTION 510 BC

DIONYSOS

Persian Soldier

ⓐ

ⓑ

ⓒ

ⓓ

Romans

ⓗ

ⓖ

ⓕ

ⓔ

ⓘ

thonged
Sandal

sole pattern

27

Greek Costume Application
A Midsummer Nights
Dream

Fairy

goat skin

Bottom

Puck

Helena

Demetrius

painted
decoration
paint
before
pleating

Hippolyta

Theseus

Roman Costume Application.
Coriolanus.

clasps

cut 2

The Woman's Tunic. The width varies according to the amount of folds required.

side seam

2 head-dresses of buckram or stiffened felt

plastic tops

c.f & c.b folds

This is the shape of the toga-experiment for size.

Toga
(not to scale)
fold line

coiled cord

stick cap to felt base

screw cap

finish with paint or spray.

stitch felt base to garment

Volumnia

Virgilia

ⓑ

ⓒ

Menenius

ⓐ

ⓓ

Young Marcius

29

ROMAN COSTUME

Drapery is a very important aspect of Roman costume and gives a sculptural and statuesque appearance to the wearer. Pattern is of very little importance, but decorative clasps are used to fix drapery, and the neck openings and sleeves of the Roman lady's dress are trimmed with braid.

Next to the skin the man wears a sleeveless shirt, over which goes a tunic worn in a variety of lengths. Over the tunic, the toga is draped (page 27, *f*), although sometimes it is worn alone. Only working people went out of doors in the tunic alone. The size of the toga is surprising and impressive: elliptical in shape and folded lengthwise, the length was three times the width and the width twice the height of the wearer. For theatrical purposes this would be unmanageable and is neither necessary nor desirable.

Women wear the stola, a long tunic-like garment, looped and draped over a girdle (page 27, *c*); it could have wide or tight sleeves. The palla, a kind of voluminous cloak, square or oblong, is added for outdoor wear, and a veil, fastened to the back of the head, falls over the shoulders at the back (*i*). Hairstyles are also shown here (*h* and *i*).

Various types of sandal are depicted for both men and women, but boots are usually seen only on men.

Application

A familiarity with Roman costume is necessary for several of Shakespeare's plays, and the suggestions on page 29 are for *Coriolanus*. The drawings show Volumnia, a Roman matron, her daughter Virgilia, a younger woman, and the young boy Marcius. The male character Menenius wears the toga (*a*). Volumnia (*b*) wears a palla over her tunic (note the use of clasps to fasten the shoulders and sleeves, and the diagrams showing how to make them). The headdress into which her hair is piled adds to the dignity of her age, and her head veil is fastened into the crown of her hair. The younger woman (*c*) has a sleeveless tunic, bound at the waist to make an overfold. She too wears the head veil, a very becoming piece of drapery. The boy's tunic finishes above the knees and he wears sandals with thonging (*d*).

The pattern given for the women's tunic must be adjusted in length according to the way it will be looped – so calculate this carefully before cutting. Experiment with the toga and discover by trial and error how large it needs to be to drape satisfactorily.

MEDIEVAL COSTUME

Good reference material is easy to find for this period. The life of ordinary people is recorded in lively manner in illuminated manuscripts, and for those who are not within easy distance of a museum, libraries can provide plenty of material and are a rich source of reproductions. Also there are brasses in old churches to be looked at and tombs where the sculptured figures can be studied in the round. In the illuminated Books of Hours, hunting, music, dancing and romantic scenes in gardens show the rich leading pleasant, decorative lives – but the poor too had their fun and there are pictures of dancing on village greens, fairs and general merriment at festivals, which suggest that both peasants and townsmen enjoyed a variety of amusements as well as working in their fields and orchards.

The cut of the clothes is simple and was governed by the width of the cloth and

Medieval.
padded head roll with wimple ►

simple head veil ►

(a)

bag hat ►

(b)

fur trimmed cap ►

2 monks

(c)

quilted tunic ►

(d)

(e)

hooded cloak
felt hat ►

note c.b. seam ►

(f)

31

Medieval Patterns

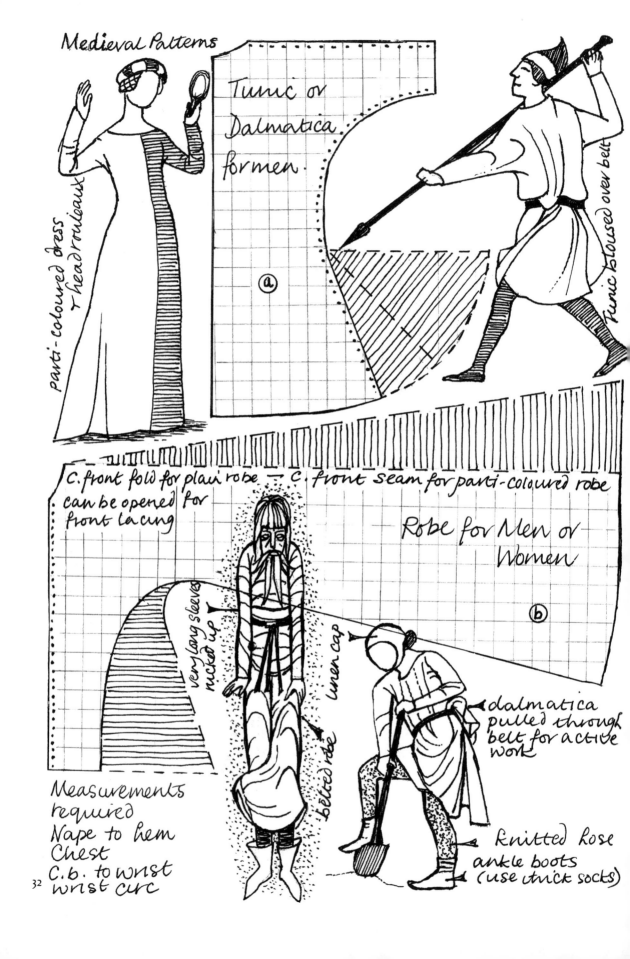

parti-coloured dress + head rouleaux

Tunic or Dalmatica for men.

ⓐ

Tunic bloused over belt

C. front fold for plain robe — C. front seam for parti-coloured robe
can be opened for front lacing

Robe for Men or Women

ⓑ

very long sleeves rucked up

linen cap

belted robe

dalmatica pulled through belt for active work

Measurements required
Nape to hem
Chest
C.b. to wrist
wrist circ

knitted hose ankle boots (use thick socks)

Application
Canterbury Tales

device

tabard worn over armour

(a)

(b)

(c)

doctor's cap.

doctor on his rounds ►

aromatic posy

dark veil worn over a fine linen veil

(d)

(e)

beaver hat

cloak

embroidered surcoat

robe pulled into pleats at waist

note belt with purse

(f)

(g) A squire

A monk with fur trimmed sleeves

petti- coat

pointed poulaines

(h)

33

the avoidance of extra seams and the need, in the case of poor people, not to be wasteful. By the fifteenth century the dresses of the rich were extravagant both in the quantity of material used and in the embroidery and rich fabrics brought back from the Middle East by crusaders as spoils for themselves and their ladies. The long, pointed, elegantly shaped headdresses with floating transparent veils, known as hennens, became fashionable, reflecting a Syrian influence.

Examples of medieval dress on page 31 pinpoint some useful details:

(a) A rich man in a pleated gown, wearing a chaperone or kind of turban which he appears to be in the process of rewinding. Note the purse on his waistbelt.
(b) Two monks, one with his hood thrown back.
(c) Another rich man whose wealth is shown by his fur-trimmed cap and the dagged decoration on his sleeves and hemline.
(d) A worker; his tunic is quilted for warmth and he wears clumsily-made shoes. Another worker (f) in jerkin and tights, is labouring in an orchard.
(e) A very simple dress and cloak. The sleeves of the dress are turned back to show undersleeves. Note the fullness gathered at the neck.

Application
Page 33 shows some costumes for a pageant based on Chaucer's *Canterbury Tales*. The Prologue gives excellent costume information, and manuscript drawings of the period show many suitable characters. Suggestions here include (a) a Knight, wearing a striped surcoat over chain mail (this can be effectively made from knitted string and a metallic spray paint); (b) a Prioress; (c) a pilgrim, with staff and scallop shell; (d) a doctor; (e) a monk; (f) a woman in a wide hat who fits well the description of the Wife of Bath; (g) a daintily dressed squire; and (h) a merchant in motley with forked beard.

Patterns for two simple medieval garments are shown on page 32. The tunic (a) can be above the knee, knee-length or calf-length. When the skirt is swung at the side (shown by the shaded area) it is known as a dalmatica – this allows more freedom of movement and scope for draping. The robe (b) can have various sleeve lengths and also hanging sleeves. When swung on the front seam, the garment may have the extra fabric pulled into pleats and controlled by a belt.

THE RENAISSANCE

From the late fifteenth century there gradually develops a more square outline, familiar from the paintings of Holbein. In the woman's dress (page 14, c) the bodice lengthens and boning is introduced. Sleeves are turned back to reveal the sleeves of the shift. The cartridge-pleated skirt is ground-length. The man's stiff, sleeveless coat with square collar illustrated on page 14 (f) is worn over a tunic which, though knee-length, is similar in shape to the woman's dress. Breeches are tied over stockings with ribbons, shoes have square 'bun' toes and slashings and puffings are being introduced.

Fashionable Elizabethan dress was both complicated and costly. This was an age of exaggeration for both men and women – bodies are both long and stiff, sleeves often enormously puffed at the shoulders, skirts immensely wide over farthingales, men's doublets padded into a distorted peascod shape. The use of stiff brocades and silks emphasizes the rigidity which is characteristic of the costume of these years. Tights or silk stockings flatters the man who has a good leg to show off.

The most markedly individual item of clothing, for men and women, which distinguishes the Elizabethan period is the ruff, a circle of elaborately pleated fabric which surrounds the neck and frames the head. It can be quite small and neat or it may be so large as to resemble a cartwheel spreading out across the shoulders. It may be edged with lace or embroidery, sometimes including pearls and jewels, or it may be crisp and plain. Often it stands higher at the back of the neck, and this is achieved by wearing a small padded bolster to prop it up. Sometimes, instead of a ruff, a gauzy collar wired so that it will hold its shape and position is worn, and serves the same purpose as the ruff in effectively framing the head. At the end of the period the ruff loses its stiffness and becomes a soft collar, anticipating the neckwear of the seventeenth century. Simpler townsfolk wore small ruffs of linen and the countryman had usually to be satisfied with a simple collar.

Ruffs are not difficult to make providing the material is carefully measured and marked before starting, and the work is deftly handled and kept fresh and clean. First stitch both edges by hand into pleats in the chosen pattern (page 36, *a*), then run threads through the inner edge (the side next to the neck) to draw the pleats in to the correct neck circumference, and finally stitch the inner edge to the neckband which has been marked accurately with the pleat distances.

A really elaborate Renaissance outfit can only be tackled by an experienced costumier, so simpler solutions may have to be resorted to when dressing Elizabethan productions on a budget. For reference and study choose some of the less spectacular costumes; there are plenty of these to be found and they can be very pleasing. Some examples are shown on pages oo–oo. For women, whenever possible, use hip pads or rolls which are easier to wear than the farthingale. If a farthingale is essential it can be made from a child's hoop with a calico cover (page 37, *b*). Use the hoop to draw the pattern; the length of material required must be a little more than the circumference of the hoop plus seam allowances. Cut from this four gores, and join the seams, leaving a placket opening. Make a channel on the long side to take the hoop, and gather the shorter inner edge and stitch to the waistband. Cut the hoop and thread it through the channel, then rejoin it and, finally, stitch tapes to the waistband. Always be sure to allow extra length for skirts that are to be worn over farthingales, rolls or hip pads; it is necessary to add several inches depending on the amount taken up by the width.

Padding for the man's peascod doublet can be built on to a tightly fitting jersey foundation (such as a T-shirt or vest; see page 36, *c*). It is easier to build it up in layers of foam rubber (which can be fixed with a suitable adhesive) or of synthetic wadding stab-stitched together. (The wadding gives a more sympathetic finish.) The trunk hose can be built up in a similar way on a pair of swimming trunks. Cover the padding with calico. The padding must be completed before cutting out the doublet pattern (page 37, *d*) as it will be necessary to take measurements of the actor wearing the padding.

Throughout the period slashing was used for decorative effect; it also allowed for freer movement in these very tight-fitting garments.

The loose coat (page 37, *e*) and pattern (*f*) can be sleeveless, showing the puffed undersleeve (*x*) in the drawing or with a puffed sleeve stitched or tied into the armhole with thongs showing a tighter undersleeve (*y*). The coat should be of a fabric that will hold a stiff shape.

Page 36 (*g*) shows a woman with hanging sleeves. Her low neckline is filled in with a gauzy partlet. On page 37 (*h*) the lady also has hanging sleeves, caught together at the

Elizabethan Costume

semi circular cloak

hip roll.

hip pads

1616

gauntlet glove

apron

peasant woman washing clothes with tucked up skirt

a smocked sleeve

net partlet

epaulettes

Jersey cotton vest

build up peascod shape with padding

swimming trunks

pearl ropes

cambric backing

construction of ruff

pleating for ruffs

Elizabethan Costume.

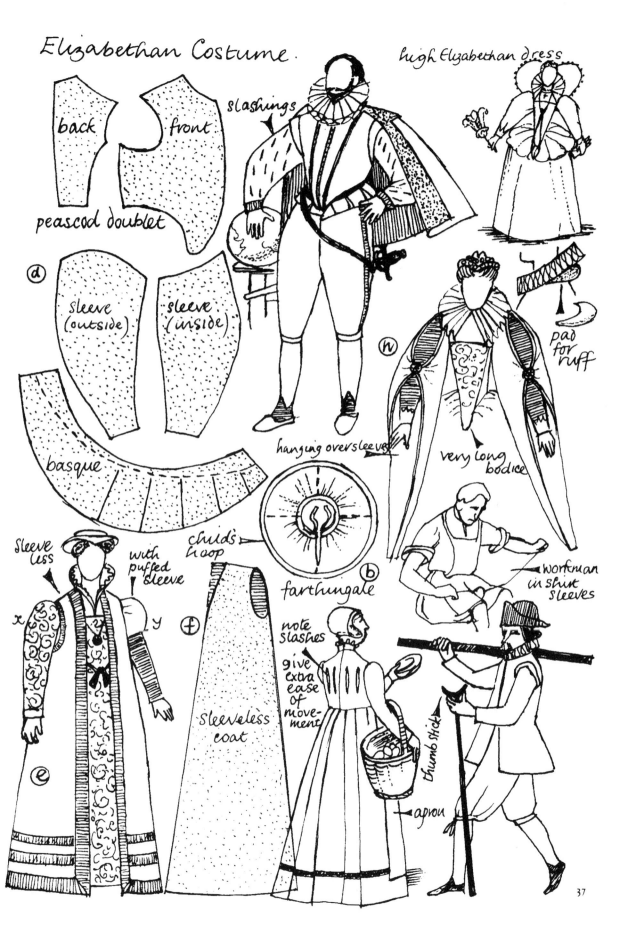

high Elizabethan dress

back

front

peascod doublet

slashings

ⓓ

sleeve (outside)

sleeve (inside)

basque

ⓝ

hanging oversleeve

pad for ruff

very long bodice

sleeve less

with puffed sleeve

x

y

ⓔ

ⓕ

child's hoop

farthingale

ⓑ

sleeveless coat

note slashes give extra ease of movement

workman in shirt sleeves

apron

thumb stick

Elizabethan application

note purse to collect money

Richard Tarlton Elizabethan Comedian.

@ anklet with bells

b turtle or polo neck - good base for collars + ruffs

add epaulettes

add cuffs

add basque

boned stomacher

hooks on underside

line for eye loops

loops

elastic

ties

head rouleau with flowers

wreath

c

stencil for dress

rosettes for shoes

front with rosettes, and she wears her ruff open at the front – a frequent practice by ladies wishing to show off their sexual attractions.

Applications

Productions of Elizabethan plays often end with a 'merry round', and the popularity of dancing, whether a stately pavane or a merry gigue, together with the singing of madrigals, maypoles on the village green and mummers at Christmas give ample opportunity for a light-hearted adaptation of Elizabethan dress. The drawing on page 38 of Richard Tarlton, a famous comedian and clown of the time, shows him making a tune with a whistle and drum – possibly accompanying dancers. Of the two men cutting a caper (*a*), the one with bells round his ankles is a Morris dancer; draperies (possibly hanging sleeves) give an extra attraction to his costume and movement.

On the same page, the diagram (*b*) shows how to convert a neatly fitting (preferably silky) sweater into a doublet by adding cuffs, epaulettes, a basque and decorative braiding. It could be worn with trunk hose or breeches. The turtle neck can take either a ruff or a collar.

The young women dancers (*c*) have stiffened bodices with boned stomachers (see page 112 for bodices). Mark out the shape of the stomacher on the bodice, make a line of loops at each edge and stitch hooks to the back of the stomacher to coincide. (Alternatively, if the bodice and stomacher are sufficiently stiff, it may be easier to use strips of velcro instead of hooks and eyes.) Their ankle-length skirts are worn over hip rolls. The dresses can be decorated by braiding, stencilling or appliqué (see chapter 8). One performer wears a formal ruff; the other has one made from three gathered layers of ribbon-edged organdie stitched to a neckband. Make use of ribbons and flowers to emphasize a rustic atmosphere.

THE SEVENTEENTH CENTURY

Historically this was a rather disturbed time; religious controversy, especially, created a divide between people which was reflected in the opulence or plainness of their dress. The silhouette varies considerably during the period but, in the main, dress is more graceful and flowing than in Elizabethan times. Elaboration is emphasized by the use of rich, mostly unpatterned, fabrics with beautiful lace for collars and cuffs (much of it of English manufacture), edgings and embroidery of seed pearls, and extensive trimming with ribbons – rosettes, bows and loops. The shape was influenced mainly by the Dutch.

Interesting accounts both of life in general and of costume are recounted in the diaries of John Evelyn and Samuel Pepys; the latter, being the son of a tailor, had an acute eye for style in dress, both for men and women. There was a marked difference between rich and poor, town and country, and the style of country dress is often that of the previous century or even medieval in character.

Except during periods of repressive Protestantism, this was a great century for playgoing, comedies being the most popular form of drama, and for the first time women appeared on the public stage. Both costumes and scenery were lavish. A taste for instrumental music developed, and musical evenings are recorded in many paintings and drawings of the time as well as domestic and rural scenes and interiors. Painters to look out for are all the Dutch masters – Vermeer, Terborch, Hals, Metsu, Steen and Van Dyck. Many minor painters depict charming scenes of country and small-town life, including some delightful skating pictures.

The Seventeenth Century.

a rich lady

sleeve ruffle

lace edged collar

1630

fur collar

40

The Seventeenth Century.

A doctor.

1662

Townswoman with muff

note curled locks with ribbon bows

Boy playing whip top

peasant's shoe

Soldier defending himself

Beribboned nobleman with bucket boots

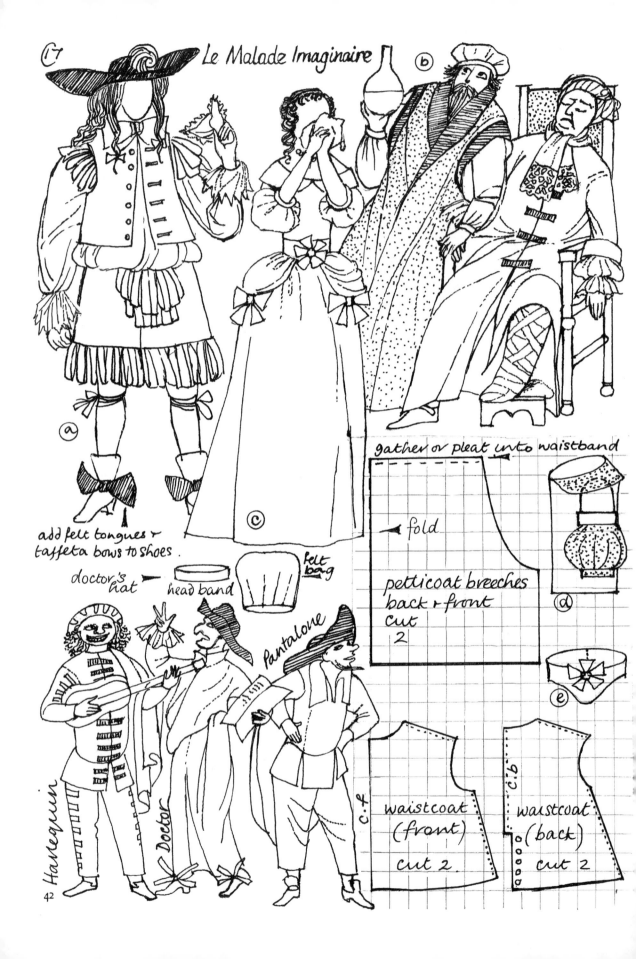

Le Malade Imaginaire

17

a

b

c

d

e

add felt tongues &
taffeta bows to shoes.

doctor's
hat

head band

felt
bag

gather or pleat into waistband

fold

petticoat breeches
back & front
cut
2

Harlequin

Doctor

Pantalone

c.f
waistcoat
(front)
cut 2.

c.b
waistcoat
(back)
cut 2

Application

The Commedia dell'Arte, whose popularity was at its height in seventeenth-century Europe, had a profound influence on playwrights – Congreve and Molière spring immediately to mind. The costume style of the Commedia is worth studying (see the figures of Harlequin, Doctor and Pantalone on page 42); it relies on shape, sometimes grotesque, to explain character and enhance action, something which is often desirable in costumes for seventeenth-century plays, in which many of the characters are highly exaggerated.

Shown on page 42 are four characters from Molière's *Le Malade imaginaire*. First, Cléante, a fop (*a*), much beribboned, wears petticoat breeches and a sleeveless jacket. The patterns provided on the same page are very simple. Add looped ribbons and a soft shirt with full sleeves; the lace cuffs can be made separately, on elastic. The doctor (*b*) wears a dark, sleeveless academic robe over a full-sleeved shirt and the typical cap or hat of the medical man. The Invalid himself (seated) has a loose, opulent dressing gown and a lace-edged jabot casually tied at the neck. A turban is wrapped round his wigless head.

For an easy version of the wife's dress (*c*) use a tight-fitting short-sleeved top (cotton or silk jersey) with a wide neckline over simple boned stays. Add a collar and puffed sleeves of organdie (*d*) and a shaped waistband (*e*). An overskirt is looped up over the silky petticoat and trails at the back.

Supply plenty of dainty lace-edged handkerchiefs for action and gestures!

THE EIGHTEENTH CENTURY

The eighteenth-century woman's dress is notable for the expansion of the skirt sideways, sometimes to a vast size, supported by hoops or panniers made of cane or whalebone. The construction could be folded forwards to ease the wearer's passage through doorways. The front is always flat, and in many cases for rich and poor alike an apron is worn – a serviceable one for working people and a rather smaller trimmed and decorated one for the rich lady. In English dress particularly there is a feeling for the pastoral, though even in the over-elaborate French court Marie Antoinette was playing at milkmaids. During the early part of the century, brocades and rustling silks are much favoured, but as the years progress there is a drift towards lawns, muslins and crisp cottons with sprigged designs – which can be represented by free painting or stencilling. A charming variety of muslin caps is worn indoors and out, and very pretty straw hats abound, trimmed with ribbons and laces.

The tricorne hat, large, small, tall, flat, braided or feathered, is the hallmark of the man's outfit. The body of the coat, in cloth, silk or brocade, is close-fitting and worn variously buttoned; the skirt varies considerably, falling closely to the hips or swinging out at the side seam in a number of pleats. The well-dressed man always wears a waistcoat, though this may be missing in a working man's outfit. Knee breeches are worn with white or flesh-coloured stockings, shirts have full sleeves, and cravats are tied in various ways. Footwear may be black buckled shoes, or boots are often worn. Contemporary portraits are an excellent source of reference on all these points.

Application

The examples on pages 45–6 have been chosen with a production of *The Beggar's Opera* in mind, but all of them could easily be adapted or used for other productions. They are

C18 Dress.

patterned fichu

smock

soft lace frill

blackbag for hair

straw hat

straight, stiff long waisted bodice

lacing across stomacher

man's shoe

housewife

lady's shoe

The staymaker.
(after Hogarth)

hessian top boots

44

C18 Costume Research & adaptation.

The Beggar's Opera

kerchief

hip pads

chemise

black coat

@

scarlet vest

1746

light cotton kerchief.

mob cap

breeches

c.f

black felt hat stiffened with shellac

add felt or leather tongue to shoe

rag clothes with nutmeg grater.

45

ⓐ

embroidered
net cap

Queen Anne doll.

cravat

cravat

cf

English salt-glaze
figure c.1730

lady's
shoe

Mrs Peachum

belt

ⓑ

canvas
gaiters

cf

hessian
boots

man with eye patch

46

C18 Patterns

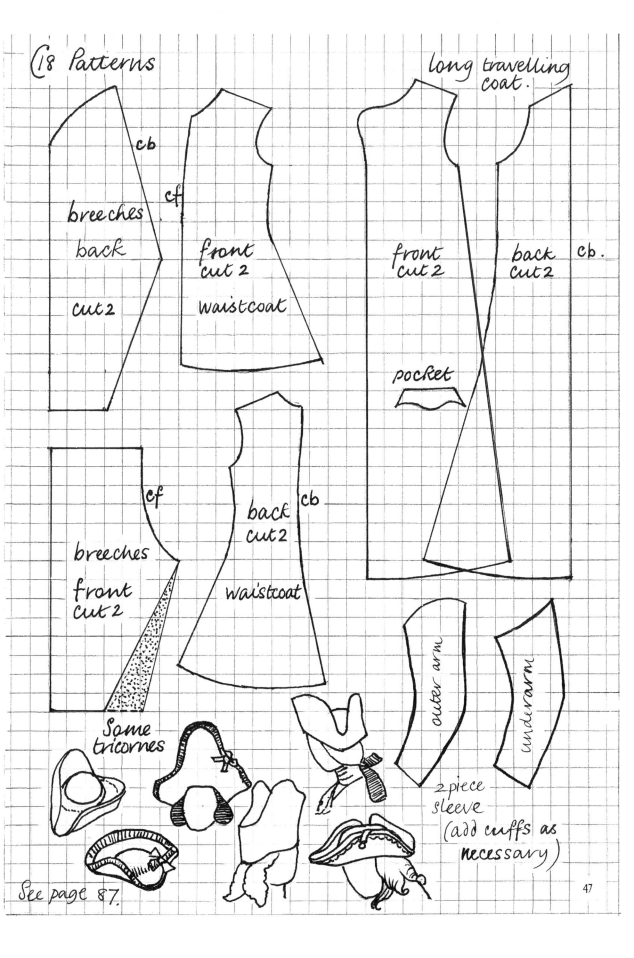

long travelling coat.

breeches
back

cut 2

cb

cf

front
cut 2

waistcoat

front
cut 2

back
cut 2

cb.

pocket

cf

breeches

front
cut 2

back
cut 2

cb

waistcoat

outer arm

underarm

Some
tricornes

2 piece
sleeve
(add cuffs as
necessary)

See page 87.

47

The Regency.

a fearsome madame

man's evening buckled shoe

brown cloth coat

(a)

straw hat

fur muff

(b)

country lass skirt tucked up to show petticoat

chambermaid at an inn

(c)

ball gown. lady wears long gloves

(d)

couple wearing walking dress

(e) lattice bonnet

(f)

selected not only for their character quality but also because they would be easy for the less experienced costume maker to construct. The good but simple shapes convey the spirit of the eighteenth century without relying on complicated cutting.

Whenever possible it will be best to use the actor's own hair, waved, puffed and set to style. Hair can be rolled over puffs of net or lambswool and fixed with hairpins. If the hair is too short a hairpiece will often help; it will have to be hired, as will wigs. For very theatrical and exaggerated productions, witty wigs can be made from horsehair or tow sprinkled with paint.

An early edition of *The Beggar's Opera* gives brief descriptions of the costumes. Only Macheath has costume changes; details worth mentioning are (1) he wore leather breeches – a character touch, and (2) his last dress was a suit of black. Peachum has a scarlet waistcoat trimmed with gold lace and a black velvet coat and breeches, similar to the figure on horseback (page 45, *a*). On the same page are ladies of the town and low male characters. Page 46 shows further ruffians; the two dolls make charming sources for Polly and Lucy; and the small saltglaze figure is Mrs Peachum to the life! The long travelling coat (*a*) is a dramatic garment which would be admirably suitable for Macheath. The figure below (*b*) suggests Macheath's prison costume – black as in the original production, neckwear in disarray, a turban protecting the wigless head.

THE REGENCY

At the beginning of the nineteenth century and during the Regency in England (1811–20) a reaction from eighteenth-century formality gave rise to the most revealing dresses ever seen in western Europe. Fabrics were transparent and flimsy, the cut was very close and, for the ultra fashionable, it was not unknown for dresses to be worn wet to make them more clinging and add to the sculptural appearance. The high waistline – just below the bust – and the long straight lines of even the less exaggerated gowns, inspired by ancient Greece, reflect the influence of the classical revival in architecture at this time (page 48, *c*). Colours were very pale with elegant classical edging. Patterned fabrics were mainly sprigged, with the use of stripes for seaside dresses.

The male silhouette is also narrow, the height exaggerated by skin-tight breeches or pantaloons. The cravat (as on page 48, *c*) is immensely high, almost throttling the wearer, and the top hat puts in its first appearance in the form we know today (*a*).

Women wear all kinds of hats, bonnets and caps; a round straw hat, tied with a scarf, gives the effect of a bonnet (*b*). Shovel-shaped bonnets (*e*), various caps and even a small coif-like head scarf (*f*) are worn. Jewelry is modest. It should not be difficult to choose a hairstyle that can be achieved using the actress's own hair. In some styles the hair is very short.

Application

For this period I have chosen a dramatization of *Pride and Prejudice* (first published in 1813). In all Jane Austen's novels comment on dress is frequent and observant.

Two of the daughters (page 50, *a* and *b*) wear a very simple and easily made version of the dress (see pattern on page 56); the channel for the drawstring is immediately under the bust and when drawn up the fine gathers can be attractively arranged both at the front and the back. The dress on the right is made without the drawstring and the

The Regency. Application - Pride & Prejudice

caléche

notched collar

ⓒ

ⓐ

ⓑ

ⓓ

Lady Catherine de Burgh

Jane

Elizabeth

Darcy

Mrs Bennet

ⓔ

fur trimmed velvet cloak

Some OUTDOOR garments

hooded Spencer

ⓕ

spencer

Mr Bennet

extra fabric is drawn in and controlled by a laced belt; loops at the underarm seam will be needed to hold the belt in place.

The older characters wear clothes which still have a late-eighteenth-century flavour. Lady Catherine de Burgh (*c*), in outdoor dress, wears a pelisse with the front edges folded back (for pattern see page 56, *b*); spikey ruffles and pleating emphasize her character, as does the huge hood (calèche) which covers her large frizzed hairstyle and adds size and importance. Fussy ribbons and a long-tailed fichu seem suitable for Mrs Bennet (*e*) who, like all married or older ladies, always wears a cap. For the elegant Mr Darcy (*d*) a striped waistcoat (vest) showing below the coat has fobs dangling from it.

THE NINETEENTH CENTURY

The loose moral attitudes of the Regency period, reflected so well in fashionable dress, disappear after about 1820 to be followed by the more constrained and rigid outlook of the rest of the century which produces respectable, enveloping and constricting garments. Men's clothes tend to become increasingly dark and stuffy and ladies, taking to corsets again, are more and more tightly laced and, from the waist down, enveloped in petticoats, crinolines and bustles. Only in the evening does the lady expose her flesh to view in a large expanse of shoulder and bosom rising seductively above the tight corsage. At times a pretty ankle and silk shoe peep from below the full skirts. In the second half of the century the invention of aniline dyes introduces some rather harsh and garish colours.

The silhouette for both men and women changes constantly, with new shapes evolving from one another quite rapidly – a foretaste of the swift progression of fashion to follow in the twentieth century. The small figures on pages 52 and 53 span the period and should help to explain some of the changes taking place. There is abundant reference material available: in addition to the mass of fashion plates covering high fashion, the excellent social information to be gained from the drawings and engravings of Cruikshank, Leech, Du Maurier and many others is helpful and instructive, showing how clothes looked on ordinary people as well as those in the forefront of fashion, and providing an enlightening commentary on current vagaries. The birth of *Punch* magazine in 1841 opens up a splendid panorama of life both above and below stairs.

The drawings here aim to show some of the less elaborate and intricate styles and some details which, when added to a simplified version of a garment, will add a touch of character and invention. The advent of tailoring in men's dress presents quite a problem when the services of a tailor may not be available – but the use of braided slipovers can provide an answer, particularly in more stylized productions. A basic pattern is given on page 56, with some ideas for its adaptation shown in the drawings *a*, *b* and *c* on page 52. The waistcoat pattern on page 57 can be used under a coat but also for characters for whom a costume consisting of waistcoat, shirt and trousers is appropriate. Shirts tend to have very full sleeves (see the carpenter, page 52, *d*). Cloth-topped boots, often worn, can be simulated by wearing spats over an ordinary shoe (*e*), and boots can have tops added to them (see page 54). Various forms of well-tied neckwear are a great aid to character – and although the top hat is almost uniform for the well-dressed man, there are all kinds of caps and shapes of hats that can be used for diversity.

The woman's skirt during the nineteenth century is variously supported by wire and whalebone frames, some of which are very cumbersome. Smaller skirts can be worn over a construction of stiff net or nylon crin (page 53, *a*), a petticoat with tiered flounces,

The Nineteenth Century.

1830 **1840** **1850** **1865** **1885**

d.b. frock coat

unstrapped trousers.

Cloth topped boots

1879

Carpenter 1830 Note full shirt sleeves + large armhole

black jersey with black silk braid

Add tails for frock coat.

white polo neck with tie

(a)

(b)

(d)

Rector at a church picnic

cloth topped boot

note casual neckware

white polo neck with silk scarf.

2 gentlemen at a music hall

(e)

spats - make from felt

(c)

The Nineteenth Century

1833

1845

1868

1875

1885

spotted net eye veil

1863

ruched muslin blouse with bishop sleeves

matron lady's cap. Make from lace doyleys

1833

mourning bonnet 1872

apron front 1878

drawstring bag

striped silk skirt

Bow for a sash

waist belt

c.f. and side bones

2 bustles from stiff nylon net or milliners crin.

ⓐ

ⓑ

straight petticoat 1880

train buttons on

Nineteenth Century

hat with cap underneath

leather fastening

watchman 1828

1860

Two Swells

Seaside boater 1800

quilted collar & cuffs

1847

getting dressed

navvy

1878 Aesthete

add tops to boots

1885

sailor

Countryman in straw hat & smock

54

Nineteenth Century.

1838

1834

(a)

back view

(b)

1827

(f) linen collar

(e)

(c) black silk + jet beads 1885

A waterfall jabot

cloth rosette + tassel

apron front

(d)

1869

Patterns – The Nineteenth Century.

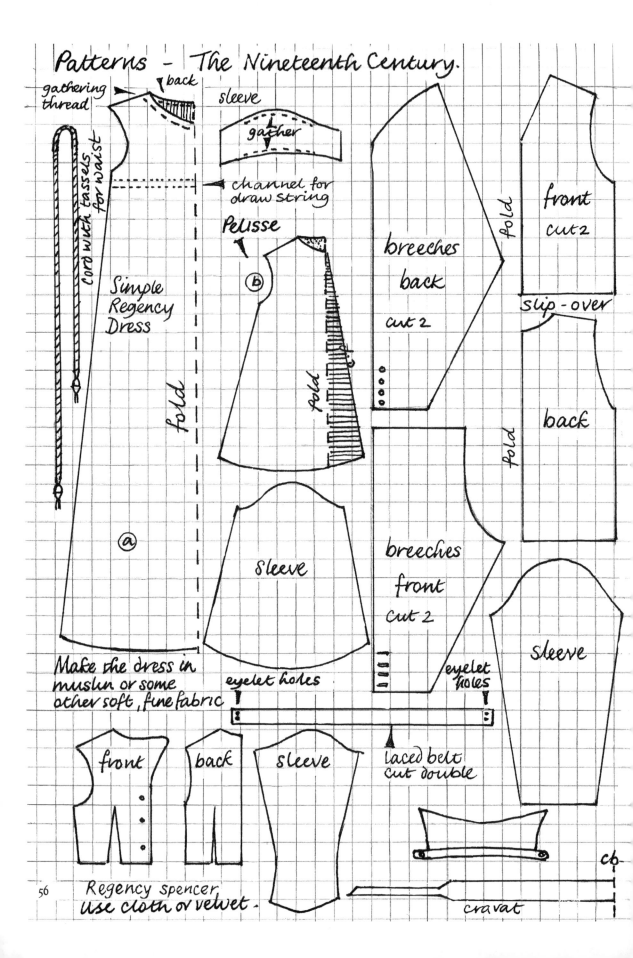

gathering thread

back

sleeve

gather

Cord with tassels for waist

channel for draw string

Pelisse

ⓑ

Simple Regency Dress

breeches back

cut 2

fold

fold

front

cut 2

slip - over

back

fold

sleeve

fold

ⓐ

sleeve

breeches front

cut 2

Make the dress in muslin or some other soft, fine fabric

eyelet holes

eyelet holes

laced belt cut double

front

back

sleeve

sleeve

Regency spencer use cloth or velvet.

cravat

cb

C19 Century Application - Nicholas Nickleby 1838.

quilted smoking cap

Smike

black neck stock

silk dressing gown

turkish shaped silk pantaloons

Mr Mantalini

Mr Ralph Nickleby

channels for draw strings

note frilly cap worn under bonnet

stomach padding

Mr Pugstyles

ties

Mrs Squeers

knitted gaiters with welted tops

Mrs Crummles

fichu pelerine

knitted fanchon

Front

b

waistcoat

c.b.

c.f.

Calico back

tapes to tie.

appliqué ribbon stripes

a

Kate Nickleby. 57

or simply by several layers of well-starched petticoats. The fullness in these petticoats must be correctly arranged: if most of it is to be at the back a flat panel at the front will be required. With all petticoats it is best to ease the gathers into a basque, in order to reduce the bulk of the material around the waist; the basque can have a laced opening so that stock petticoats can be adjusted to different waist sizes. Petticoats may also be made with extra flounces or trains that can be buttoned on to the hem when necessary (b).

Throughout the period the position of the waist departs more or less from the natural waistline, sometimes being marked by a sash, belt or cummerbund. Towards the end of the century it is forced very low by a cuirasse bodice. Corsets control the shape, but it is possible to adapt blouses, neatly darted and/or slightly padded, to achieve an acceptable line, especially if they are worn with boleros, shawls, a pelisse or a fichu (see page 55, a to d). Jackets, pelerines and mantles (e) and (f) are easily constructed and look charming over a well-shaped skirt.

Application

On page 57 the drawings are taken from an original copy of Nicholas Nickleby with contemporary illustrations by Phiz which I have chosen as a source for this costume application. Here is a mine of information with the added bonus of marvellous characterization and spirited presentation. This illustrated series of Dickens' novels should be consulted by any designer about to produce costumes for a Dickens dramatization or for readings in costume. Just a few characters are shown, with some details which may be helpful. As most of the costumes need to have a well-worn look, some breaking down of the garments with a spray gun, a little judicious painting and some rubbing with sandpaper or a cheese grater to fray the edges and show wear at knees and elbows will be advantageous.

The striped waistcoat could be painted or have appliquéd ribbon stripes. The pattern for a fichu-pelerine (a) should be made of some soft fabric which will drape nicely over the shoulders; alternatively it could be crocheted or knitted, as is the fanchon for which a diagram is also given (b). Cut a good paper pattern for the fanchon; the instructions taken from The Young English Woman 1869 say: 'Begin at the back corner, cast on 5 stitches, increase at both ends following the paper pattern. First row of pattern – alternatively knit two together, throw the wool forward. Second and third rows knitted. Finish off with a crocheted edging.'

Make the most of hair shapes (using the performer's natural hair if possible) and of characterful hats and bonnets.

FIN DE SIECLE: 1895–1910

At the end of the nineteenth century the tenor of life is changing. Travel, transport, sport, and the participation of the working classes in activities from which they had previously been excluded are all having an effect on the clothes people wear. Although there is still tight lacing for women and dresses of immense frothiness are much in evidence among the rich and leisured classes, trim skirts, blouses and jackets begin to be seen on women who are leading more active lives and leaving the shelter of the parental home for offices, factories or the professions.

Although men's formal dress is still much in evidence, the male also is frequently more easily dressed, and as sport becomes popular blazers and softer shirts emphasize a

From 1895 – 1910

ⓐ

ⓑ

ⓒ

applique or insertion bands

narrow black velvet ribbon

jabot

choker 1900

moustaches

waterproof cape cloak

net fichu

silver & enamel necklace

leg of mutton sleeve

gather

dressing gown

panama hat.

59

more casual approach – see the two figures on page 59 (*a*) watching a boat race. The same page shows a trim figure with a tailored jacket (*b*) whose plain skirt is made more interesting by the addition of tucks. High-necked blouses can easily be adapted to a period look by the addition of bands of trimming (*c*); always ease the fullness of the blouse to the front to achieve the fashionable pouter-pigeon look. All dresses and blouses are tightly waisted and this is helped by using a shaped belt, for which a pattern is given on page 61.

For shoes to be worn with light dresses, bows or buckles can be added to slippers or ballet flats; painting a design on stockings simulates the embroidered stockings then in vogue and adds further detail (page 61, *b*). The lady's walking shoe or boot is usually laced – add a felt spat to a court shoe (*a*); or, if the shoe is worn with a ribbed sock of the same colour, buttons can be added to give the look of a buttoned boot.

For men and women, caped coats and cloaks for travelling and as bad-weather and waterproof garments are popular and frequently of a check fabric. As described in chapter 8, striping with a lining fitch and a straight edge is an easy way to achieve the right effect.

Application

The page of drawings relating to the period (page 62) are for Oscar Wilde's mannered comedy, *The Importance of Being Earnest*. Although the characters belong to the area of high fashion, simple adaptations make it possible to design less elaborate costumes which still have the right quality of wit and style. A play such as this is a satisfactory subject for designing within a limited colour range – for instance, creams, mauves and greys, with a touch of black here and there for emphasis. It will give point to the stylization of characters and dialogue and the air of unreality of the plot.

Of the two women, Cecily's ribbon-trimmed blouse and skirt (*a*) contrasts with the more sophisticated redingote and smart town hat with travelling veil worn by Gwendolen (*b*). Lady Bracknell's character is accentuated by uncompromising lines, embellished with braiding and jet trimmings. John Worthing, guardian of the pretty Cecily, is formal in a frock coat, whereas Algernon, on an illicit country visit, is more casual in his smart striped suit. Canon Chasuble's clerical coat and gaiters and Miss Prism's plain skirt and bolero (*c* and *d*) are at a more mundane level.

Because of the intricacy of tailoring, it may be advantageous (and even cost-effective) to hire men's costumes for this period. They can be given a more individual touch by combining the hired garment with a made waistcoat, interesting neckwear, gloves etc. and the addition of jewelry such as tie pins and watches. Women's jewelry may often be borrowed.

1895 – 1910

trim blouse and skirt.

lady's walking boot

@

1905

flower seller

gauze ruff.

braided jacket

evening cape

knicker-bockers

skirt with braid trimming

shaped belt

travelling cloak.

evening blouse

velvet ribbon choker

61

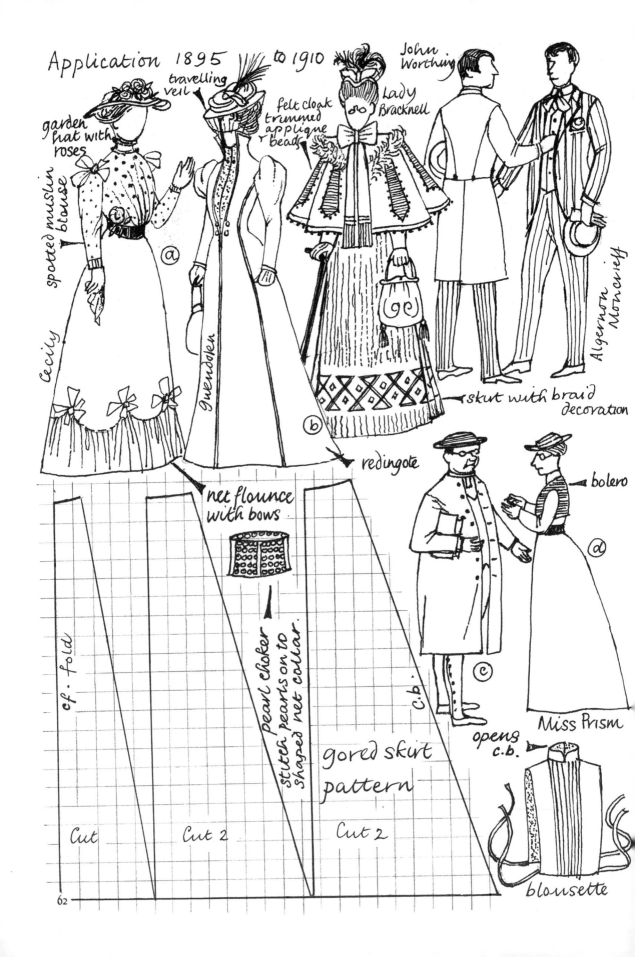

Application 1895 to 1910

John Worthing

Lady Bracknell

garden hat with roses

travelling veil

felt cloak trimmed appliqué & beads

spotted muslin blouse

Cecily

Gwendolen

ⓐ

ⓑ

Algernon Moncrieff

skirt with braid decoration

redingote

net flounce with bows

Pearl choker stitch pearls on to shaped net collar.

c.f. fold

c.b.

gored skirt pattern

Cut

Cut 2

Cut 2

bolero

ⓒ

ⓓ

Miss Prism

opens c.b.

blousette

1910 to 1939

silk flowers

hat pins

1921 evening dress

1921 day dress

1910 ingenue

1910

1922

b

flower sellers

1911 morning suit

1922

a

on the beach 1929   on the golf course

63

The pouter pigeon look with narrowed skirt and top-heavy bust, fashionable at the turn of the century, is made even more top-heavy by enormous hats – secured by very long and often decorative hat pins, sometimes with knobs at both ends for extra security – the second knob being screwed on. (Elastic hat-guards are also worn.) The skirt reaches its narrowest extreme in the hobble (page 63, *b*) in which the wearer was hardly able to put one foot in front of the other. For sport more freedom was necessary, so skirts, although still tailored, become wider and clear the ankles.

Shorter skirts, which had made a temporary appearance during World War I, reappear about 1920, and a straight line, much more simple in cut, replaces the earlier complicated seaming. From ankle length, skirts rise steadily till they reach the knee in the mid twenties when the dress becomes a mere tunic with the waistline dropped to the hips. The close-fitting cloche hat (page 67, *a*) tightly covers the helmet of hair and frames a painted face. Fabrics are commonly geometrically patterned, suitable for a jazz-age society frenetically enjoying itself.

From 1929 the skirt begins to drop again and as it goes down the waist rises and the shapeless boyish figure is replaced by more revealing lines. Dress materials are used on the bias, stretchy fabrics such as crepe are much in vogue and the cutting becomes more intricate. The emergence of trousers for women, flared or bell-bottomed, is mainly seen on the beach or for cruising (page 63, *a*).

Although men's formal dress – morning coat or frock coat – is still seen, and in the city black jackets and striped trousers are fairly uniform, the lounge suit and tweed suit, the sports jacket and blazer, are all invading the man's wardrobe. The pages of *Punch* for the period pinpoint the collar width and trouser length. Top hats and bowler hats give way gradually to softer hats (page 67, *c*), panamas for summer (*b*), cloth caps (page 65, *a*), and there are many occasions, particularly at the seaside, when the boater is still popular. Stiff collars gradually lose popularity to more comfortable soft ones as the years go by.

Application

An Evening with Noel Coward: the drawings on pages 68 and 69 are for well-known musical numbers from productions by Noel Coward whose work for the theatre spans the years covered in this section. Designs need to be light, witty and imaginative and should be easy to wear by both dancers and singers.

The first drawing on page 68 is an adaptation of a Poiret design in a spectacular fabric – a good opportunity for some fabric printing. The wrap is fastened with a barbaric clasp (*a*). A chiffon cloak for a dancer (*b*) is easily made from two squares of chiffon or a similar floating type of fabric (see pattern on page 69). The four points are tapered and gathered at the ends into silk tassels which should have a dress weight inserted into the knob to give enough weight for the cloak to hang well. Character costumes for 'Runcorn' (*Fête Galante*) are built up from 'found' stock dresses, in this case lacey knitted jumper suits rescued from second-hand clothes shops and doubtless worn just after World War I by respectable aunts.

Moving on to the middle of the twenties, the juvenile lead (*c*) wears a blazer and flannels; this is an excellent opportunity to adapt the slip-over pattern, painted with stripes and braided. His partner's dress (see pattern on page 69) could be made in a light linen or heavy crepe and is trimmed with bands of lace, either appliquéd or inserted. (To insert the lace, stitch it to the dress before cutting away the background fabric.) The inverted side pleats give extra room for movement.

1910 - 1939

smoking jacket

1914

paisley silk collar + cuffs

1911

woollen cardigan

middle class walking dress 1911

@

1913

dowager's shooting party hat

one piece blouse 1911

long strands of pearls are very popular.

note trouser crease

fold

front

sleeve

back

cuff

1914 motoring spats

This lady wears a tie

65

For the 1930s (page 69) the girl (*a*) wears jersey bell-bottomed trousers. The typical striped top of the period can be adapted from a T-shirt, over which is worn a skimpy matching jacket; a large-brimmed straw sun hat completes the outfit. The group of dancers (*b*), taking part in a wartime Coward number, anticipates the next section; their character costumes are made up of found items. (Note that they each carry a gas mask case, as everyone in England during World War II was obliged to do.) It is important, when using pieces from stock, to assess them when grouped together for colour and style and make sure they form a cohesive whole.

WORLD WAR II

With nearly all the young men and women in uniform, and increasing shortages and regulations, the war years are rather static as regards dress. People resorted to make-do-and-mend and alterations, together with desperate invention, to cheer up their wardrobes. Small items that required few clothing coupons, such as headscarves, became fashion items. Those who resented using valuable coupons for stockings used leg paint as an alternative. Government regulations in Britain limited the yardage used in garments, and utility clothing, with its familiar marking (page 70), was introduced as a further measure to help the war effort. Women took increasingly to trousers for work, for wear in air raid shelters or simply for keeping warm.

FROM 1945 TO 1980

The continuation of clothes rationing prevented any immediate flowering of fashion in Britain at the end of the war and most people had to wait a few years before dressing with complete freedom. Young people and students, in particular, took advantage of cheap army surplus clothes, such as duffle coats and sheepskin flying jackets. When the fashion industry revived and new styles became available again there was still much more conformity than there is today. The hem length became an important fashion point, and women altered their skirts accordingly. Greater availability of fabrics encouraged once again a feminine look and gave rise immediately to fuller, longer skirts inspired by Dior's 'new look' (page 72, *a*). The A line (*b*) and the pencil line (*c*) followed in fairly rapid succession. But just as the man in the street was still expected to wear a suit on many occasions, most adult women possessed a country tweed or a town suit, although hats were much less worn than before the war, by both men and women.

It is not possible to describe here the development of dress since 1945, but the drawings on pages 72–74 indicate some of the more prominent fashions. It should be borne in mind, however, that many people were influenced very little by the constantly changing fashion scene, as a glance at the shoppers in any High Street today, with their straightforward coats and comfortable shoes, makes apparent. Factors that have affected everybody's attitude to dress in the past fifty years have been the introduction of many new types of synthetic fabric, the change in the manner of fastening to zippers and Velcro, nylon stockings and tights, the popularity and practicality of blue jeans, and the use of plastics, particularly in rainwear and footwear. Drip-dry and non-iron fabrics, together with washing machines in the home, have revolutionized the care and maintenance of clothes; and the wide availability of low-priced fashion garments 'off the peg' has meant a great decrease in home dressmaking.

1910 – 1939

Party cloak with quilted collar.

school cap

a

japanese parasol. 1927

bare backs are popular

panama hat

1929

1928

towelling bathing wrap

farm worker

working man 1930

b

1925

c

knitted waistcoat

plus 4 outfit.

stencil design. 1931

tweed suit

1930s turn-ups.

1927

67

An evening with Noel Coward

net ruffled collar

chiffon wrap.

ⓐ

ⓑ

slave bangles

'I'll follow my secret heart.'

long gloves

'Dance Little Lady'

choir boy - 'Runcorn.'

ski pants braided down side seams.

'Try to learn to love'

'Some day I'll find you'

ⓒ

slip over painted stripes & braiding

white cricket flannels

2 Spinsters

lace appliqué or insertion

co-respondent shoes

'Runcorn'

An evening with Noel Coward

Mad dogs & Englishmen

solar topee

bush shirt

baggy khaki shorts

brogues

1920's

Flattening bust bodice

sports shirt

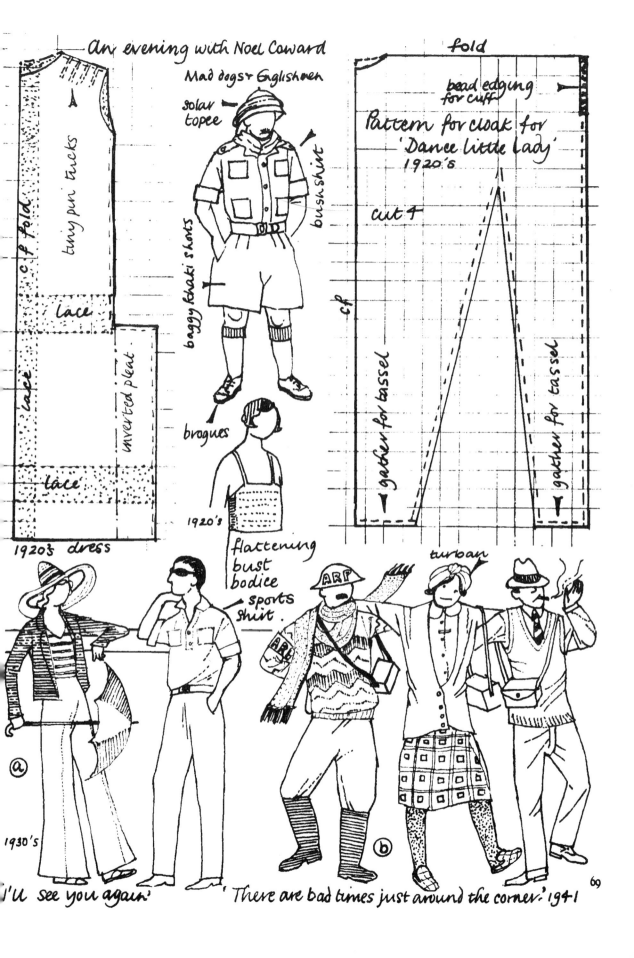

cf fold

tiny pin tucks

lace

lace

lace

inverted pleat

lace

1920's dress

fold

bead edging for cuff

Pattern for cloak for 'Dance little lady' 1920's

cut 4

cf

gather for tassel

gather for tassel

turban

ARP

ARP

ⓐ

ⓑ

1930's

'I'll see you again'

'There are bad times just around the corner' 1941

69

World War II CC41

chenille snood

shirt from striped dusters

leather belt from 2 dog collars

siren suit

fire watcher

wedge soled shoes

A.R.P. Warden 1941

durndl skirt from curtain fabric

cape from grey blanket

corduroy trousers

knitted hood

gasmask

printed scarf

striped crêpe evening dress

evacuees

land girl

factory worker

70

For most contemporary plays and some reviews and dance numbers, it is cheaper and more sensible to buy costumes than to make them. The occasional requirement of a couture garment of high fashion may necessitate cutting and making something special and the latest fashion magazines should be consulted for ideas. A fashion designer is better for this job than a theatre designer; there is a difference in out-look, and the theatre designer often does not grasp the current trend and image in the same way.

For modern plays where the fashion element is not important, second-hand clothes will be a cheap answer. Charity shops are a likely source; they vary in their type of merchandise, and a shop in an up-market area will often carry fashionable clothes whereas other shops are excellent for character garments.

Performers may be able to provide suitable clothes themselves, but it is usually helpful to supply some little addition or detail that will assist the actor to feel that he or she is playing a part.

Postwar – 1945–60

ⓐ

walking length umbrella

ⓒ

1958 sack

sneaker

business man

business man

1955

ⓑ

1949 tent coat

summer dress

ballet flats

velvet trimmings

permanently pleated skirt

girl playing netball

duffle coat with hood.

film camera man – duffle coat & woolly hat

1954 Teddy Boy

1960 – 1980

flowery tie 1965

black r white wool Jaegar dress 1966

Platform soles 1973

A white ribbed stockings

see through net

sun dress 1966

sunglasses 1964

1968

clinging ribbed polo sweater 1970

hot pants

Crocheted dress black thigh boots

denim jacket

body stocking

long black leather coat

1975

light-up necklace 1975

flared trousers

1966

jeans

Paco. Rabanne dress 1962

the army look

beehive hair do

73

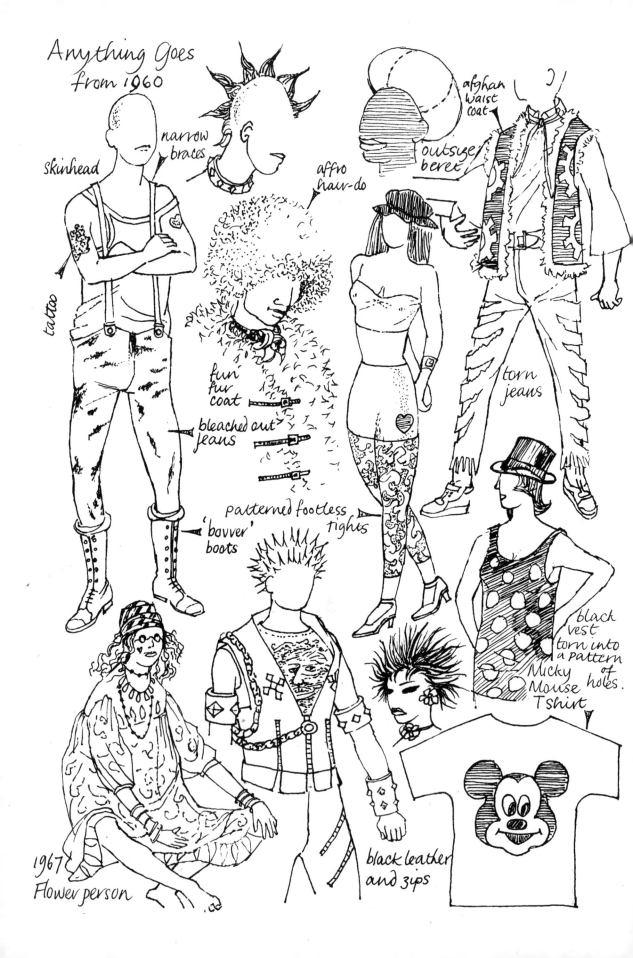

Anything Goes from 1960

skinhead

narrow braces

tattoo

affro hair-do

afghan waist coat

outsize beret

fun fur coat

bleached out jeans

torn jeans

patterned footless tights

'bovver' boots

black vest torn into a pattern of holes.

Micky Mouse Tshirt

1967 Flower person

black leather and zips

4 Choosing and making accessories

The addition of a *well-chosen* accessory, in many instances, will complete a costume. It is necessary to emphasize the words 'well-chosen' because accessories added in haste can be the ruination of a costume which was until then satisfactory. Accessories will not save poorly conceived designs but they will add point and finish if they are well thought out and appropriate; guard at all times against fussiness! Accessories can also enhance a character and may help the performer in his or her role.

Some details will add to the look of a finished garment; some, such as spectacles or walking sticks, will add character; and some are needed for 'business'. The latter are often called for at short notice by a director whose attitude is that anything will do – and the actor may also be satisfied with the first thing that comes to hand. Beware of actors adding details of their own choice without the designer's knowledge. It is the designer's responsibility to see that every item called for will look right, is to the right scale and is in keeping with the design as well as being practical to use.

Practicality is very important – it is no good providing handbags that do not open, spectacles that fall off or anything that is difficult to handle. Make sure that costume props are available for rehearsal so that actors can become familiar with them and discover any snags. It is important to be sympathetic to the actor's problems.

Accessories and costume details may be made specially or they may be found. Sometimes the found items need repairs or some adaptation or addition, and if the colour is wrong they may have to be sprayed or dyed, or need additional paint. It should be instilled in performers and stage managers that all accessories must be carefully handled and cared for during the run of the production.

Finally, when the run is over, props and accessories should be overhauled and packed away carefully in labelled boxes.

Many found objects, discarded trimmings and costume jewelry, can be recycled in the making of accessories. When you visit market stalls and junk shops, keep a look-out for possible treasures. The following ideas and methods for making accessories may prove helpful.

Walking sticks The cockerel walking stick (page 76, *a*) is a long stick which tapers to a point. Model the bird's head in plasticine on to a short length of broomstick, one end of which has been drilled to take the thicker end of the walking stick (*b*). Cover the plasticine with several layers of torn paper and paste and, when dry, sandpaper gently. Glue the stick into the hole in the head section and bind with tape to make a satisfactory join. When all is dry, paint and varnish.

For a knobkerrie, (*c*) find or make a knobbly stick. With some scrumpled wire mesh make a good shape on the top of the stick. Cover this with paper mâché and paint when dry. Finish off with two rubber washers.

For a hooked cane (*d*), choose a good stick, drill a hole in the top and push into it some strong wire, bend over to form the handle and bind with tape. Soak the tape in glue and bind tightly with rope or coarse cord, winding it closely round the handle and then continuing to twist it down the stick, spacing it out as you go. Find a plastic ferrule

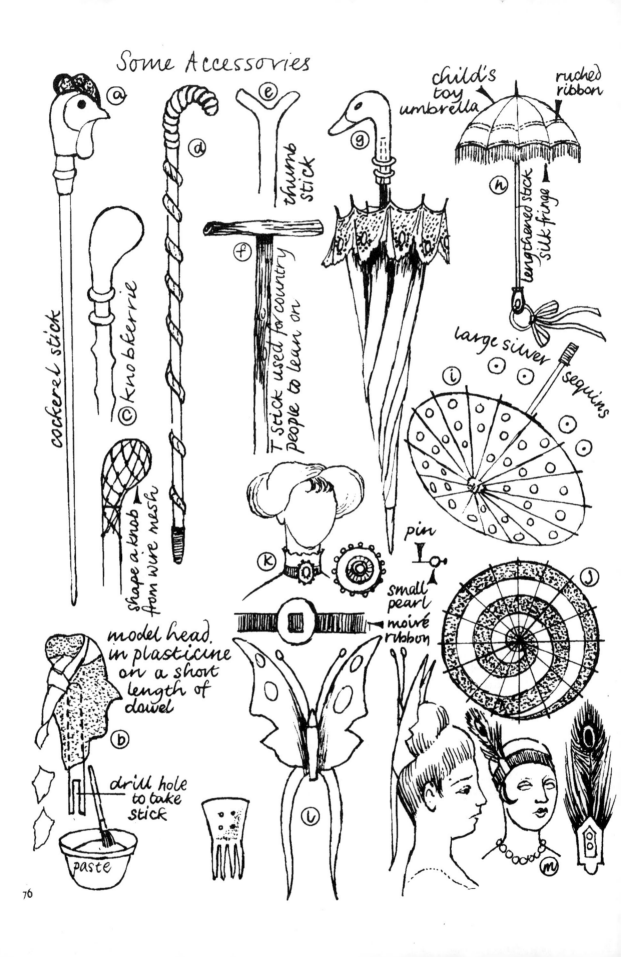

Some Accessories

cockerel stick

(a)

(c) Knobkerrie

Shape a knob from wire mesh

(d)

model head. in plasticine on a short length of dowel

(b)

drill hole to take stick

paste

(e)

(f)

thumb stick

T stick used for country people to lean on

(g)

(i)

pin

small pearl

moiré ribbon

(k)

(l)

child's toy umbrella

ruched ribbon

(n)

lengthened stick

silk fringe

large silver sequins

(J)

(m)

More Accessories

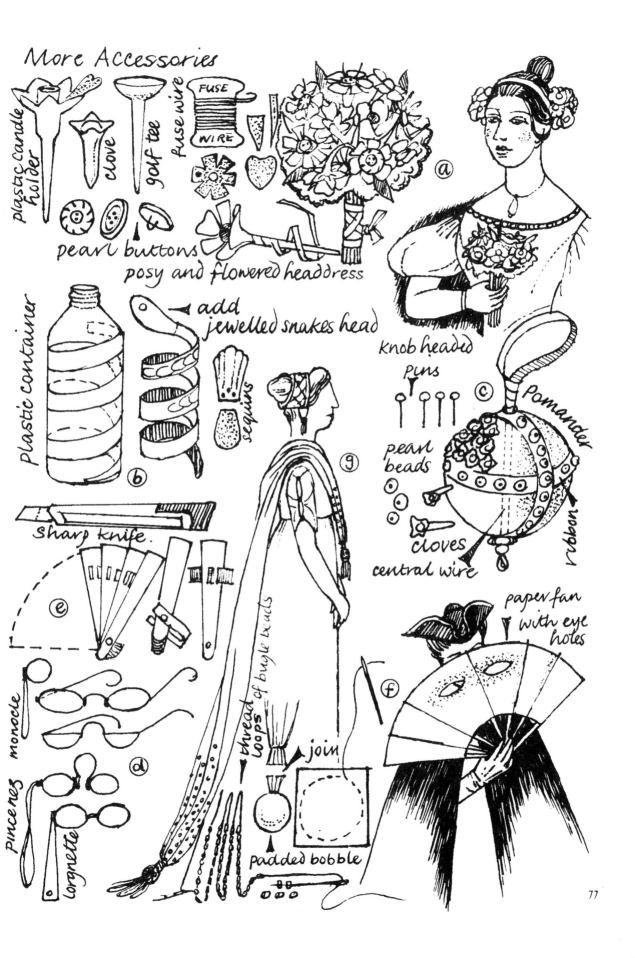

plastic candle holder

clove

golf tee

fuse wire

FUSE WIRE

pearl buttons

posy and flowered headdress

ⓐ

Plastic container

add jewelled snakes head

sequins

ⓑ

knob headed pins

Pomander

ⓒ

pearl beads

cloves

central wire

ribbon

Sharp knife.

ⓔ

ⓖ

Pince nez

monocle

lorgnette

ⓓ

thread loops of bugle beads

join

padded bobble

paper fan with eye holes

ⓕ

(many plastic bottles have tops which can be adapted) and fit this to the pared end of the stick. Paint and varnish. If it is not possible to find a suitably shaped thumb-stick (e), push wires into the top of the stick to make the V shape and cover with papier mâché. The handhold of the T-stick (f) is fixed to the staff with a large screw.

Umbrellas For a Victorian umbrella (g), model a duck's head onto a short length of broomstick as in (a). Cut the handle off an unwanted umbrella and insert the shaft into a hole drilled in the broomstick. Paint the handle, and trim the edge of the umbrella with soft lace.

Victorian and Regency sunshades (h) were very small. A child's umbrella can be adapted by first lengthening the handle, then trimming the parasol with very soft ruched ribbon and a silk fringe edging.

For dancers or a chorus, Japanese parasols can make a spectacular effect: (i) is spattered with large silver sequins while (j) is decorated with a painted spiral.

Jewelry For an Edwardian choker (k), cut two slots in a circle of firm card and thread onto a moiré ribbon, then glue an identical circle on top of the first. Find a suitable plastic bottle cap and glue it to the centre, and on this fix a pearl or coloured bead. Round the edge arrange a ring of small pearls held in position by knob-headed pins passed through them and inserted into the edge of the cardboard rings (or use pearl-headed pins), and finish with paint. If available, use a tiny buckle to fasten the ribbon, or failing this a small plastic press fastener.

The butterfly decoration, for a hairstyle in which the hair is piled on top of the head, (l) is made from wired net or gauze, from acetate or even from thin card. Wire or sew it to a hair comb in which holes have been drilled, and add ribbon or fabric streamers. Another head ornament, this time for a short, neat 1920s hairstyle (m) consists of feathers fixed to a clip which can be attached to a bandeau.

More accessories (illustrated on page 77)
Small, pretty flowers reminiscent of Victorian wax flowers can be made from the items shown (a). Cut paper petals and small leaves. Using a contact adhesive, assemble the flowers, mounting the petals on cake-candle-holders, golf tees or cloves, with pearl buttons or seeds or grains for the centres. Attach the flowers to wire stems bound with green tissue paper. Put the flowers and leaves together to make a small nosegay, surrounding it with lace or a white paper doyley and binding it with ribbon. Smaller bunches attached to a wired headband can be used as a headdress to be worn with a ballgown – or for a bridal wreath the flowers can be arranged round a circlet. In each case use a small brush to spatter white emulsion and gold paint liberally to give a waxen finish.

For the snake bangle (b), choose an arm-sized plastic bottle and carefully draw the spiral as shown with wax pencil. Then cut very carefully with a sharp blade. Also cut a snake's head, and glue it to the spiral with contact adhesive. Paint the spiral with a neutral coloured emulsion paint; when it is dry, glue onto it overlapping scales made from suitably shaped sequins or cut from scraps of leather or plastic cloth. Lightly brush the completed bangle here and there with bronze or gold paint. A solid, flat coat of gold will look artificial and tawdry.

A pomander (c) was frequently carried in the sixteenth and seventeenth centuries. Base it on a polystyrene ball of the kind used by flower-arrangers, or a child's hollow rubber ball. First fix two lengths of stiff gold or brown braid or ribbon round the ball as shown. Then push a firm wire through the centre so that it protrudes about 40mm (1½ ins) at the bottom, thread on to this a couple of wooden beads and make a loop of the remainder of the wire using pointed-nosed pliers. Make another wire loop at the top, bind it with ribbon and glue this in place, and then make a ribbon loop. Insert cloves into the ball between the ribbons (it may be necessary to pierce holes in the rubber ball with an awl). Fix pearl beads into the binding braid with knob-headed pins. As with the bangle, lightly brush over the pomander with bronze or gold paint.

A selection of spectacles (d) should, if possible, be collected from second-hand stalls. Period shapes vary and are usually much smaller than modern ones. Spectacles can be adapted to make a lorgnette with the addition of a handle. Monocles have an adjustable circumference and are worn on a cord and tucked into a waistcoat pocket.

A small fan can be made from acetate sheet (e). Make the struts according to the diagram and carefully punch a hole in the narrow end of each of them. Put two aside. Carefully cut three slits in the others and thread a length of very soft ribbon through them as in the diagram. With a plain strut at either end, insert a rivet through the punched holes leaving it loose enough to allow some movement, and glue a sequin on each side to stop the slats slipping off. When this glue is quite dry adjust the slats on the ribbon and glue the ends of the ribbon to the end slats of the fan.

A charming fan (the original is in the Armoury Museum in Moscow) with eye holes cut into it (f), is amusing and mysterious.

The neo-classical stole (g) is worn over one shoulder, short at the front and trailing on the ground at the back. The softly falling fabric should be about 450mm (18 ins) wide tapering at the ends to about a third of this width. To make the large glass tassels, use two squares of fabric, mark out circles for gathering threads, fill the circles with wadding and add a dress weight or something heavy before drawing each one up tightly. Gather the ends of the stole and stitch to the spare material on the tassels, binding the join with matching silk or cord. Thread bugle beads onto a long thread and make a number of loops, stitch these to the base of the tassels and finally cover the round part with bugle beads.

Sample Costume Plate

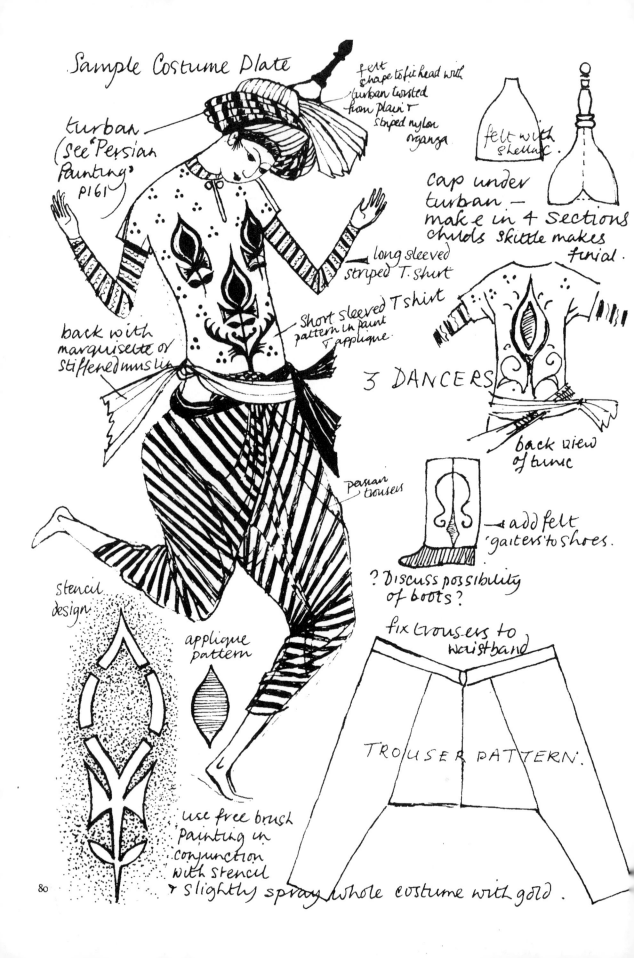

turban
(see "Persian
Painting"
P161)

felt shape to fit head with turban twisted from plain & striped nylon organza

felt with shellac.

Cap under turban — make in 4 sections childs skittle makes finial.

long sleeved striped T.shirt

Short sleeved Tshirt pattern in paint & applique.

back with marquisette or stiffened muslin

3 DANCERS

back view of tunic

persian trousers

add felt 'gaiters' to shoes.

? Discuss possibility of boots?

fix trousers to waistband

stencil design

applique pattern

TROUSER PATTERN.

use free brush painting in conjunction with stencil & slightly spray whole costume with gold.

5 Thinking about design

To create a performer's costume there has to be a design. Designing a costume does not necessarily involve producing a drawing or painting on paper, although this is a sound way to clarify the designer's thoughts and to present ideas to the rest of the team for discussion. An alternative method is to build a costume on the performer, choosing existing items from the wardrobe. The selection and putting together of components to create a whole is a perfectly valid design process. For some modern costumes, character costumes and groups of extras needing background co-ordination without heavy outlay, this is often the best way to work.

First, of course, the piece to be performed must be studied in depth, whether it is drama, opera, dance or some other event such as a pageant or carnival, for this is the springboard from which all ideas evolve. Several important factors should be considered at this point, namely:

1. the budget for the production, and its implications (see chapter 2);
2. the style of the production and its setting, to be confirmed in discussion with the producer and set designer;
3. the length of the run of the production and the consequent wear and tear on the costumes;
4. the time factor that governs designing and making.

Style arises from holding a point of view and having an awareness of visual things, looking at a wide range of visual themes and selecting and discarding various aspects according to the requirements of the production. Designing is not copying from a chosen source but a process of assimilating and synthesizing the information you have gathered into something new and relevant.

Ideas can be drawn from different styles of painting; for example, look at works by Stanley Spencer such as *The Resurrection*; by Seurat (already used as a source for *Sunday in the Park with George*); Chagall; some of the very theatrical and decorative paintings of Burra; the colours and shapes of figures in industrial settings by Lowry; the strange shapes and configurations of Hieronymus Bosch. Try to find Grandville's *Animals, the World's Vaudeville*; he was a superb nineteenth-century French illustrator with a marvellous eye for costume shapes and amazing headpieces. Even today's *Comic Strip* is a style which could be used for inspiration.

For the more traditional needs of a historical background, paintings, prints and photographs of the period will be the main source material, remembering always that choice is paramount and that through selection it is possible to achieve a synthesis which will convey the magic of the theatre rather than pedestrian everyday life! In addition to pictorial material, museums and galleries can offer sculpture, pottery, tapestries, weavings and much else to furnish exciting ideas – ethnic art is often very inspiring. Keep scrap books and files of useful postcards, cuttings and information. Sometimes the preliminary idea for a design can be triggered off by a piece of fabric or a scrap of trimming; riffling through a collection of oddments may set off an interesting train of thought. The best advice on research is: look everywhere all the time, and keep looking. There is no substitute for the trained, observant eye.

The designer who can put designs down on paper has the advantage. This can be done in a variety of ways: the choice of medium will depend on the mood of the piece. Designs carried out on flat white paper do not convey the true values of the colours as they will be seen on the stage, so it is useful to place your designs against background washes and textures that indicate the tone and quality of the set.

Before starting to draw a design, experiment for fun with watercolours, chalks, felt tips, inks or painting sticks, which can be used singly or in combination to give many interesting results. Drawing can be done with pen, brush, conté or pencil – aim to keep the work fresh and lively. Armed with this experience, ideas can be freely and fluently expressed when the time comes for starting work on a production. For those who are not comfortable with these materials or who have limited drawing ability, collage may be helpful. Cutting up an assortment of different papers with scissors and assembling the shapes on a background can give satisfactory results. If time is short, good clear working drawings or diagrams will be sufficient provided they are accompanied by explanatory notes and snippets of the fabrics to be used. Be sure to provide a back view! Complete the costume plate with the name of the character and the relevant scene as well as the actor's name. Mount the design on card and slip it into a plastic sleeve so that it will stand up to the wear and tear of studio and workroom; presenting designs on scraps of crumpled paper or the backs of envelopes is not good practice. Above all, if the design is unclear the result will be faulty – clarity between designer and maker is absolutely essential.

It is also important that good feeling should exist between the maker and the wearer of the costume – if this kind of harmony is not established, life can become very difficult and tensions will show in the finished work. It may be difficult to achieve, but it is part of the designer's job to see that it happens.

Much of the mood of the production will depend upon colour. Colour can bring out the gaiety of comedy, the darker shades of tragedy; it can flood the scene with sunlight or add to the feeling of storm and tempest. It is also vital, together with shape, in emphasizing character. It can help or hinder the performer's interpretation of his part. As an experiment, arrange pieces of coloured paper or scraps of different coloured fabrics together, move them about and judge the resulting moods they create. Try a large area of one colour against a small area of another. Play about with bright primary colours, dun colours, clear pastel colours in combination. How can they be made to glow, to recede, to accent? This can be a very helpful exercise.

A specific palette can be interesting when there is a need for a stylistic approach: black and white alone, black and white with grey or with one brilliant colour – say, yellow. Think also of using a range of one colour – imagine a glowing range of reds, for instance. Whatever your decision, some restriction of the palette and colour range is advisable, because too much variety and too much diversification can lead to a very fractured scene.

Finally, for drama (as opposed to spectacle or pageant), the best costumes are not those which assail the spectator's eye, which astonish, which are so important that the production and the performance become lost – the best costumes are those where the design is so right that they hardly seem to have been designed at all.

6 Costume building

If you have managed to assemble a stock of costumes during several years of dressing productions, you will have a very useful nucleus on which to build, either by adding newly-made or newly-acquired garments to existing items or by putting together new costumes entirely from wardrobe stock. This is often particularly satisfactory for character costumes, when it can be a help to 'feel' your way into the character by trial and error. It is a good method for servants, working people and country people because the results do not look too contrived. (The dye bath and sprays can be useful in this context.) An appeal for contributions to the wardrobe may bring in items that are no longer of use to their owners but have value to the designer; temporary loan can also be a useful source.

Working in this way, it is easy to see the shape of a costume develop as it is assembled on the performer – to assess the need for more bulk, more drooping, or more crispness, and to decide on suitable and agreeable colours and textures that will add credibility to the character. Sometimes it is desirable that the garments should not fit very well, and this is easier to achieve with oddments off the hanger. Looking at photographs helps to focus the way garments are assembled in real life and may point a way to doing this theatrically.

A group exercise in costume building
This is a corporate exercise in design and can be used either to create a set of costumes for a specific play – perhaps the one currently in rehearsal – or to alert the group to the motivation behind costume design and its effect on the creation of character. In either case there must be a theme – the production in view, or an idea chosen for the exercise – and a set amount of time should be decided upon for the exercise.

Spread out in a good space a glorious jumble of fabric lengths, remnants, cardboard boxes, a variety of papers and foils including strong wrapping paper, various trimmings, string and rope, polystyrene pieces, together with garments, hats, boots and shoes, stockings and tights, and some cushions or wadding that could be used for padding. There must be plenty of variety and appealing colours.

Each member of the group should be allotted a particular character or type for whom to create an original costume from the materials laid out before them. Working in pairs may be helpful. Plenty of scissors, staplers, large needles and coarse thread, large pots of paint and brushes must be available. Cardboard boxes and packaging can be used to build up shapes, headdresses or animal costumes. A condition of the exercise should be that the costumes must allow the wearer to move easily.

If the costumes are to be used for a production they should be massed together and assessed as a group so that the whole aspect, not just each individual costume, is satisfactory. In this case, it is likely that some adaptation and alteration will be needed to achieve a coherent style.

7 Garments from very simple shapes

The very simply cut costumes on pages 85–89 can be used in many different kinds of production. Most early historical costume and peasant dress is based on simple shapes but these garments will also be found invaluable in a number of other situations, especially if fabrics, colours and pattern are used inventively. Consider using them for carnivals, festivals and very way-out and zany productions. They are easy to make, easy to fit and easy to wear.

In many of the patterns, the ratio of length to width is doubled or halved; use a pair of dividers or compasses to check this on the patterns as it will make enlarging and drafting much easier. Draw patterns on squared paper so that measurements and right angles can be easily checked; if possible use squared drafting paper bought from a supplier of dressmaker's sundries. The dotted lines indicate sewing lines. It is important to check the grain of the fabric: the sign + indicates the straight grain. Trousers that have a lot of drapery between the legs should be made in soft fabrics. For other garments, decide whether the shape should be stiff or soft and choose the fabric accordingly.

There is no need for a lot of measurements, but the following are essential:

for trousers outside leg; waist to knee, calf or ankle as required
for skirts waist to knee, calf or ankle as required, waist circumference
for other garments nape to waist; nape to knee, ground etc. as required; wrist to wrist across back; across shoulders; outer arm straight. Occasionally a chest measurement is needed.

Using squares (illustrated on page 85)

(*a*) A simple coat which can also have sleeves (*b*) added.
(*c*) A burnous (a North African hooded cloak). This also makes a good garment for the medieval period or any other situation when a hooded cloak is called for.
(*d*) A very basic poncho from Mexico, with many uses.
(*e*) Basic trousers. If the trousers are sufficiently full there is no need for a gusset.
(*f*) Trousers often found in peasant costumes, and suitable for medieval country people.
(*g*) Oriental trousers, with baggy folds between the legs.
(*h*) A simply constructed peasant blouse using two squares for the body. A draw-thread from x–y can be used for a boat-neck or a closer circular neckline. Squares folded in half make the sleeves, attached at an angle as shown; they can be either straight, open sleeves, or gathered at the wrist, or shaped and tapered to the wrist.

Using circles (illustrated on page 86)

Cutting circles from fabric is less economical than working with squares.

(*a*) Circular cloaks fall agreeably and are very easy to make – an opening can be made centre front, or on another axis (*b*), when the cloak can be thrown dramatically over the shoulder. The hole for the head need not be made centrally but can be placed in such a way that the drop at the back is deeper than that at the front (*c*).

Using Squares

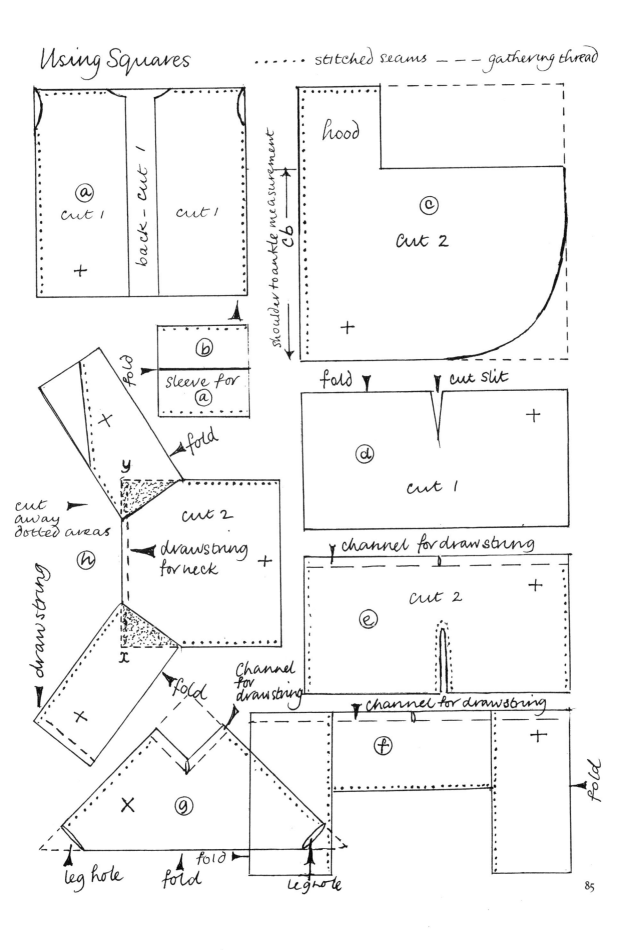

Using Squares

······ stitched seams — — — gathering thread

ⓐ cut 1   back – cut 1   cut 1

+   +

hood

ⓒ cut 2

+

shoulder to ankle measurement   cb

ⓑ sleeve for **ⓐ**

fold ▶

fold ▶

fold ▲   cut slit ▼

ⓓ cut 1

+

y

cut away dotted areas ▶

ⓗ   cut 2   drawstring for neck

+

drawstring ▼

x

channel for drawstring

ⓔ cut 2

+

fold ▲

channel for drawstring

Channel for drawstring

ⓕ

+

fold

ⓖ   X   +

leg hole   fold ▶   fold ▶   leghole

85

Using Circles

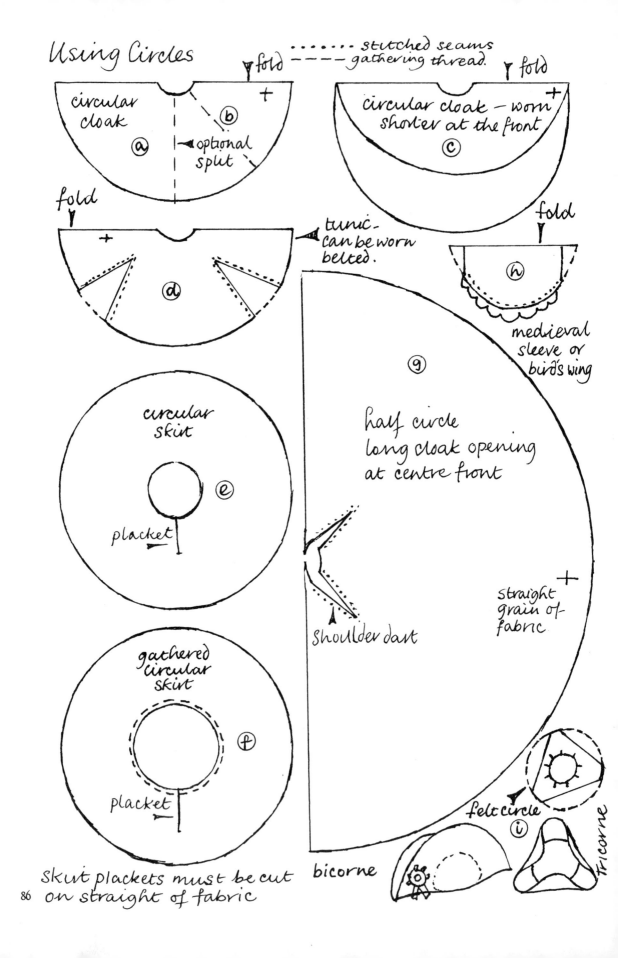

.... stitched seams
------ gathering thread.

fold

circular cloak

ⓐ

←optional split

ⓑ

fold

✛

ⓓ

tunic-can be worn belted.

fold

circular cloak — worn shorter at the front

ⓒ

fold

ⓗ

medieval sleeve or bird's wing

circular skirt

ⓔ

placket

half circle long cloak opening at centre front

ⓖ

shoulder dart

straight grain of fabric

gathered circular skirt

ⓕ

placket

felt circle

ⓘ

Skirt plackets must be cut on straight of fabric

bicorne

tricorne

(*d*) A short tunic, overblouse or dalmatica which can be worn loose or belted. The material can be pulled together in pleats, front or back, under a belt in the fifteenth-century fashion (see page 17).

(*e*) and (*f*) Two circular skirts. In (*e*) the central hole is made to the measurement of the wearer's waist and will fit smoothly on to a waistband. In (*f*) the central hole is cut larger and is gathered into the waistband. In either case a placket opening will be required. Both these skirts move nicely when worn by dancers.

(*g*) A long, half-circular cloak. This should be made of a heavy fabric such as a blanket or heavy tweed cloth. The neck should be bound; it can be fastened with a cord or tapes.

(*h*) A medieval sleeve (or a bird's wing) with a dagged edging inserted into the seam.

(*i*) From a circle of felt stiffened with shellac both a tricorne and a bicorne hat can be made. Using a felt skull cap for the crown, first cut a hole in the felt circle slightly smaller than the circumference of the cap and cut nicks in it to form tabs. Glue the tabs to the cap with contact adhesive and allow to dry. Then soak the brim and cap with shellac and shape the brim by using rolled newspaper as packing and clipping or tying the felt in position over it.

Simple garments (illustrated on page 88)

Patterns are given here for a variety of very simply contrived garments.

(*a*) and (*b*) An ecclesiastical cloak which must be made from a stiff fabric or will require lining. It must be stiff enough to hold the shoulder angle, and the back of the neck should rise to the base of the skull.

(*c*) A sleeveless peasant dress to be worn over a lawn or muslin blouse such as (*h*) on page 85. Gather the skirt x–y to fit the yoke, which may be lined if required.

(*d*) and (*e*) Two pairs of trousers: (*e*) is the shape worn in northern India and falls with many folds between the legs; (*d*) is a much straighter trouser as worn by the Chinese.

(*f*) A very baggy trouser which needs only a small gusset. All three trousers have a channel added to the top to take a drawstring, usually of a lightweight material to reduce the bulk round the waist.

(*g*) A sleeveless Chinese waistcoat with appliquéd decoration. Cut two pieces alike and make a centre-front opening.

Bold shapes

Shape, as emphasized throughout this book, is of primary importance in all aspects of costume. The drawings on page 89 rely on simple, dramatic shapes that are unfussed by trimmings and detail and make arresting statements. The silhouette is all-important. When searching for a sense of style you will find costumes such as these will not only provide inspiration but will help to clear the mind: during research, ideas can become cluttered with detail and unnecessary historical information which frequently obscure the simple view.

Using Simple Shapes.

· · · · · · · · · · stitched seams
— — — — — gathering thread.

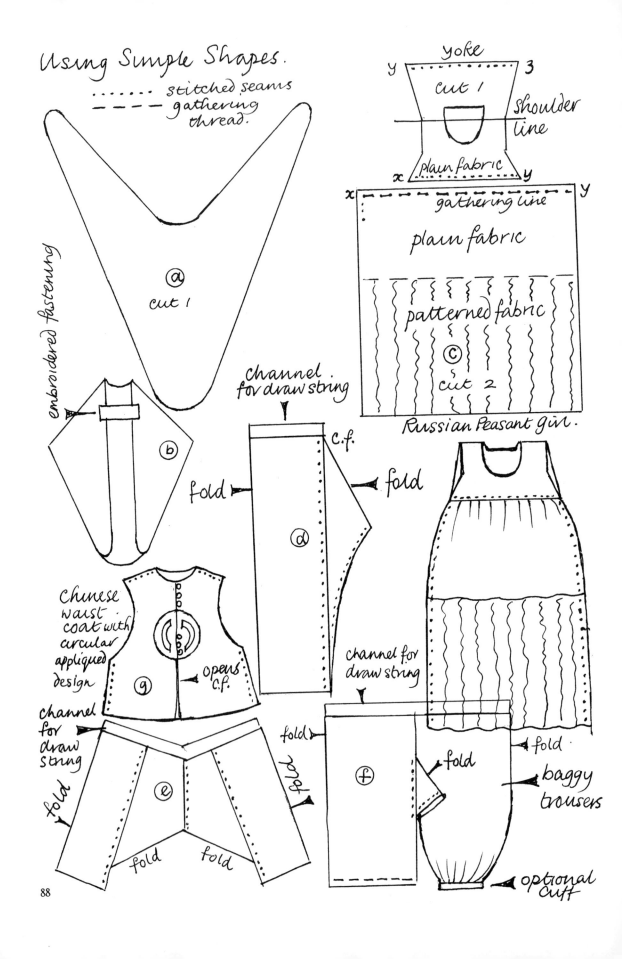

yoke
y   3
cut 1
                shoulder line
plain fabric
x   y
x   y
gathering line
plain fabric
patterned fabric
© cut 2

Russian Peasant girl.

embroidered fastening

@ cut 1

b

channel for draw string

fold ◄   ► fold
c.f.

d

Chinese waist coat with circular appliquéd design

channel for draw string

fold

e

g

opens c.f.

fold ►

◄ fold

► fold

channel for draw string

f

► fold

◄ fold

fold

◄ fold ·

baggy trousers

◄ optional cuff

88

Bold
Shapes

8 Fabrics plain and patterned

The choice of fabric is of primary importance. Even if the design of a costume is excellent and it is superbly made, the result will be unsatisfactory – or even a failure – if the wrong fabric has been used.

If there is a choice between natural and man-made fibres, in practically every case the natural fibre will behave better. A fabric made of natural fibre will fall into better folds, it will have more 'give' and, in the case of historical costumes, it has the advantage of being the type of material that would have been used at the time and is therefore likely to look more authentic.

Another important factor to consider is the weight of the fabric – whether it should be heavy or light, stiff or soft, a close or open weave, and whether it requires lining. Many period bodices are better if based on a calico lining, and some skirts need lining either to add bulk or to make them move well or fall into the necessary pleats or folds. Experiment freely until you gain the experience that comes from working with fabrics and makes the correct choice second nature. Pin different lengths of fabric in a variety of ways on a dress stand and observe the draping qualities, how a fabric stretches round the form and how it behaves on the straight and on the cross.

There will also be the question of whether to use plain or patterned fabrics. For those working to a tight budget, the following methods will transform cheap fabrics with a variety of colours, patterns and textures at minimum expense and will give ample scope for invention and experiment.

Dyeing

Commercial dyes can be used satisfactorily to achieve plain colours. Do not be afraid to mix them to get interesting results. For strong colours, boiling may be advisable: use a metal bucket or dye bath (according to the quantity of fabric) over a gas or electric ring, or an electric boiler. For paler colours use cold water dyes. (It is possible to use a washing machine for either method.) Be sure to read and understand the manufacturer's instructions.

For flat dyeing the fabric should first be soaked in cold water, to remove the dressing if the fabric is new and to ensure that the fabric absorbs the colour evenly. Most dyeing requires the use of salt – so keep a good stock available. Rinse dyed fabrics in cold water and either hang them up to drip-dry or spin-dry them in a machine. *Never wring newly dyed cloth.*

Tie-dyeing

For this method, do not wet the fabric first.

Bind twists of plain fabric with tape or string and tie off (page 92, *c*) – or tie pebbles, beads and seeds into the fabric at intervals – to form patterns; the tied parts of the fabric will not take the dye. To give extra colour and dimension to the pattern, tie-dyeing can also be done on patterned fabrics, or the fabric can be re-tied and dyed in further colours.

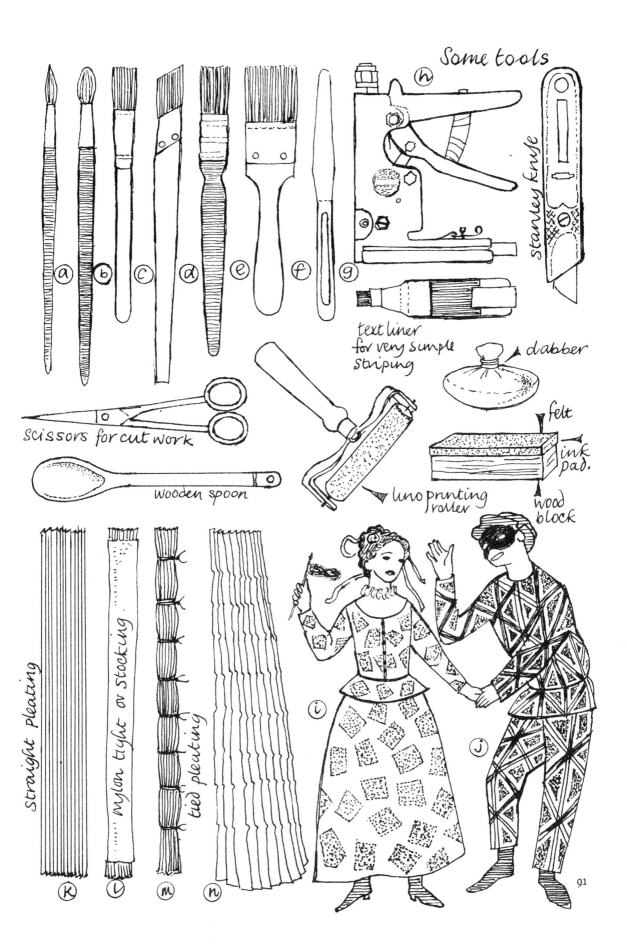

Some tools

a b c d e f g

h

stanley knife

text liner
for very simple
striping

dabber

felt

ink
pad.

wood
block

lino printing
roller

scissors for cut work

wooden spoon

straight pleating

nylon tight or stocking

tied pleating

k l m n

i

j

91

pin carefully

ⓐ

small stitch
at front

long stitch
at back

QUILTING spread out on a table

ⓑ

hank of embroidery cotton

appliqué

free
painting

tie dyeing

FABRIC
PAINT

quilted
bodice

ⓒ

ⓓ

ⓖ potato printing

petticoat
with
quilted
hem

ⓔ

ⓗ

knife

lino
cutting
tools

ⓘ

patterned
lining

quilted
child's
cap

ⓕ

Afghan merchant wearing quilted coat

Dip-dyeing

This is used to achieve a graded area of colour, such as a hemline. Wet the fabric and hang it with the lower edge in the dye bath. The dye will creep up the fabric, getting gradually paler. Remove it from the bath when the desired effect has been achieved, rinse and drip-dry.

Soak-dyeing

For an uneven and blotchy effect, suitable for fabric that is to be used for worn and ragged costumes. Use a bowl that will just accommodate the material, push the material roughly into the dye and leave it without moving it around until sufficient dye has been absorbed.

Pleating

Ready pleated fabric can be bought, or a length can be sent to a professional pleater, though the latter is an expensive process. Pleats can also be pinned or basted in place and then ironed. But for more informal pleating, try the methods shown on page oo. The fabric should be fairly soft and lightweight (but not a jersey fabric). Two people are needed for the operation, one standing at either end of the length of dampened fabric, which is then taken up and formed by the fingers into tight pleats. It must be held very firmly and then pulled hard lengthwise so that the whole pleated length is absolutely taut (page 91, *k*). A nylon stocking or one leg of a pair of tights is then fed over and eased down the full length of pleated fabric, and the resulting roll is left to dry slowly (*l*). The roll can be tied at intervals to produce kinks in the pleating (*m* and *n*). A different kind of pleat results from twisting the length of pulled pleating tightly before pulling the stocking over it. For a shaded length, dip one end into a bowl of dye and steep until the gradation is satisfactory, then allow to drip dry.

Painting and printing

All painting and printing of fabrics must be carried out on a firm table which has been padded with newspaper, a thin blanket or cloth and covered with a clean sheet.

There is no limit to the variety of design that can be painted on to fabric either with fabric paint obtainable in pots or tubes or with emulsion paint. Bear in mind that these both have a tendency to stiffen the fabric and should therefore not be used too thickly – although items such as stomachers or canvas armour may well benefit from being stiffened in this way.

Painting with dyes, or with some of the crayon products now on the market, leaves fabric more flexible. As new products are always being developed it is wise to keep an eye open for anything which may be helpful in this field.

Any kind of painting demands good brushes and these should be treated with respect, cleaned in a suitable solvent and then washed in detergent or soap and water. Page 91 shows a selection of brushes which would be useful:

(*a* and *b*) Watercolour brushes for fine and medium fine painting.
(*c*) A pastry brush: these are good-tempered, strong and above all very cheap and can be used for broader work.

(d) A lining fitch, essential for painting stripes or checks as it draws easily against a straightedge. It is also very good for stencilling.

(e) A small-size decorating brush. It would be useful to have various sizes for larger areas.

(f) A Chinese brush for broad, free work; these come in a variety of sizes and are also useful for larger areas.

(g) A plastic palette knife – much cheaper than one with a metal blade and very useful for mixing and spreading paint.

Painting design on fabric demands a more experienced artist than some other methods such as stencilling where neatness and accuracy are adequate. Even with very free designs the cloth should be lightly chalked with positioning guides, and it is wise to have a clear sketch of the design to follow. Once the brush is on the fabric *there is no going back*, so it is essential to have the design and the process clear in your mind before starting.

Stencilling

This is particularly suitable for repeat patterns. The design should be drawn on oiled stencil paper (which is non-absorbent) and cut out carefully with a sharp knife (page 95). There should be a good margin round the design and register marks can be cut along the edges of the paper. The design should be simple, because intricate shapes will soon wear out, tear away, or allow the paint to leak under fine lines leaving a messy result. Guidelines lightly drawn on the fabric will keep the pattern regular. Attention to the consistency of the paint is important: if too thick it will clog the stencil and stiffen the fabric, if too thin it will spread untidily.

Emulsion, acrylic and fabric paints can all be used for stencilling and a lining fitch as illustrated will give much better results than the brushes sold specifically for the purpose. The underside of the stencil should be cleaned from time to time with a clean rag.

Striping

When suitable striped or check fabric cannot be obtained, a satisfactory substitute is not difficult to achieve with a lining fitch, a straightedge and some paint. Striping can be carried out quite quickly by a neat worker with a steady hand. The work should be done on a flat surface, and with lighter fabrics it may help to fix them to the surface with thumb tacks or pin them to a heavier cloth. Hold the straightedge at a slight angle, and cut a notched guide to mark out the stripes. The drawing (page 95, a) shows the method for striping a late eighteenth-century polonaise. It is usually better to cut out the garment and stripe the pieces rather than striping the whole length of fabric.

Simple block printing

For very basic patterns a potato cut can be used (page 92, g), but as it wears out quite quickly it will probably have to be renewed several times in the course of one project. Apply the paint to the potato cut with a brush or dabber or use a well-primed felt ink pad. Potato prints are not suitable for heavy, rough-textured fabrics.

A design cut in lino will not wear out and can be more intricate. Linocutting tools are illustrated on page 92. The lino should be mounted on a block of wood for easier handling and it can then be banged on the back with a hammer to achieve a good impression. A lino-block is best inked with a roller.

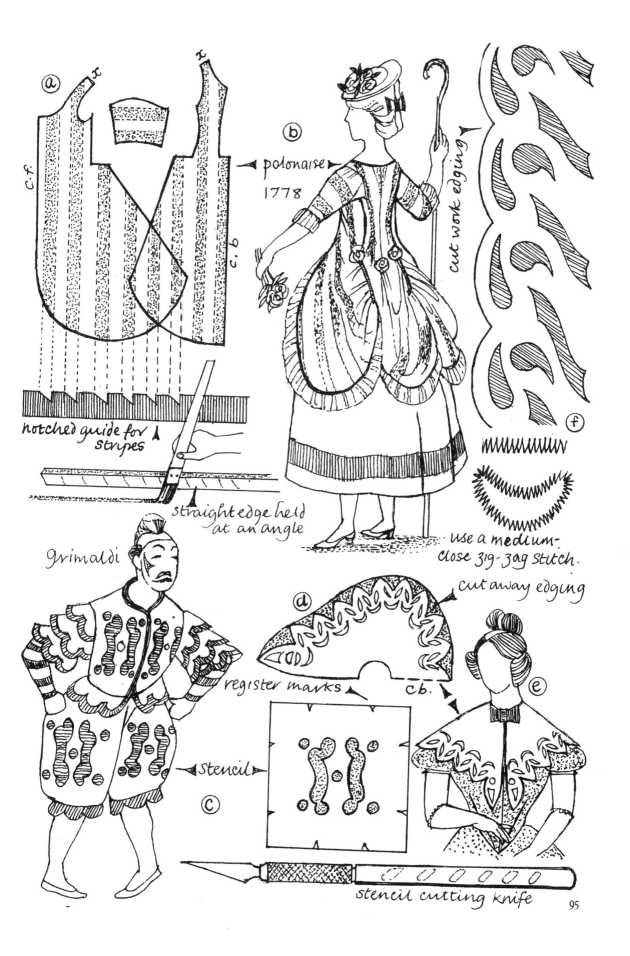

(a)

c.f.

x x

c.b.

notched guide for stripes

straight edge held at an angle

(b) ◄ polonaise ►
1778

cut work edging ►

(f)

use a medium-close zig-zag stitch.

Grimaldi

cutaway edging

(d)

register marks ► c.b. ◄◄

(e)

◄ stencil ►

(c)

stencil cutting knife

Screen Printing.

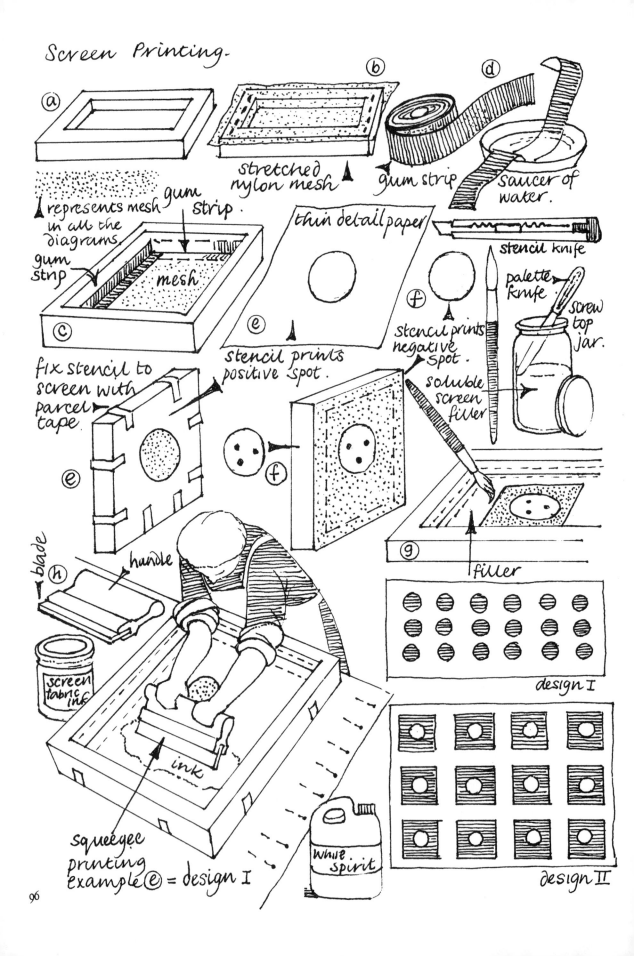

(a)

(b) stretched nylon mesh ▲

(d) gum strip ▲ saucer of water.

▲ represents mesh in all the diagrams.

gum strip

gum strip

mesh

(c)

thin detail paper

stencil knife

palette knife

screw top jar.

(e) stencil prints positive spot. ▲

(f) stencil prints negative spot.

soluble screen filler

fix stencil to screen with parcel tape ▶

(e)

(f) ◀

(g) filler

design I

(h) ◀ blade handle

screen fabric ink

ink

squeegee printing example (e) = design I

white spirit

design II

Screen printing

Screen printing is a very satisfactory way of printing lengths of cloth. The equipment is neither costly nor extensive and after the initial outlay on one or two screens and a squeegee, these items can be used indefinitely. Printing is done one colour at a time. Any number of colours may be used.

Equipment

Screens can be purchased from a supplier of art materials, but can easily be made from pieces of 1½ × 1½ in. wood. The construction must be strong and the corners good. You will also need:

Nylon mesh to cover the frame
Staple gun and staples
Brown paper gumstrip
Scissors
A stencil cutting knife
Thin detail paper for the stencils and/or soluble screen filler, often known as 'blue glue', for blocking out areas of the mesh.
Watercolour brushes, a plastic palette knife and some clean jars with closely fitting lids to hold paint.
Masking tape for use with stencils
Fabric paint specially prepared for screen printing
White spirit, Polyclens, plenty of clean *cotton* rags for cleaning the screen
A good squeegee for printing

Preparation (see illustrations on page 96)

The size of the screen (*a*) depends on the design. It must be large enough to allow a margin of no less than 100mm (4 ins) all round the design. A very large screen is heavy and cumbersome to lift; too small a screen is fiddly to handle and tends to be messy. An inner measurement of 305 × 380mm (12 × 15 ins) would be a practical size for a beginner.

The first step is to stretch the nylon mesh across the screen (*b*). Cut a piece of mesh about 75mm (3 ins) larger than the screen on all four sides; unless a good margin is allowed it is very difficult to grip the mesh, which must be pulled drum tight over the screen. Using a staple gun (page 91, *h*), fasten the mesh to the screen along one of the shorter sides, then, pulling hard, staple the opposite edge. Repeat on the other two sides. It is essential that the surface is absolutely taut. Trim the edges of the mesh neatly to the edge of the screen. (N*ote: in the drawings on page 96 the mesh is represented by small dots; this is the area which will print.*)

Now turn the screen over (*c*) and cut four lengths of brown paper gumstrip about 50mm (2 ins) longer than the inner edges of the screen. Run the strips through a saucer of water (*d*) one at a time and fit them neatly into the angle where the mesh meets the wood. Tuck the excess length at each end round the corner. Four further strips should be added, laying them flat on the mesh and overlapping the first strips, but this time abutting the frame, not angled to rise up the sides. Allow to dry slowly.

For the design, take a piece of thin detail paper and draw out the image (*e*), in this case a circle. Place the detail paper on a hard surface (a plastic cutting board is ideal) and carefully cut round the design using a sharp knife. Either piece can then be used as a stencil.

To produce design 1, using the stencil with a circle cut out of it, strap the stencil to

Pattern
Ideas.

2 tiger patterns

stencil
or screen
print.

screen
printing

Japanese theatrical
costume

indian mirror work

try
stencilling
with some
appliqué.

a young lady 1569, embroidered
sleeves. These could be quilted.

try appliqué

G7 Ethiopian. St Mark

98

G3 tile mosaic.

the stapled side of the screen with masking tape wrapped tightly over the edge of the screen (*e*). To produce design II, using the circle itself as a stencil, attach the circle to the screen with two or three dabs of soluble screen filler (*f*). In this case the filler is also used to complete the design (*g*).

Filler can be used in conjunction with paper stencils as described, or it can be painted on the screen and used by itself; in this case, draw the design on the screen and paint with the filler the areas which are not to be printed. Note particularly that paper stencils are always fixed to the side of the screen to which the mesh has been stapled, whereas the filler is always painted on the inside of the screen, as in illustration (*g*). The filler is water-soluble and can be washed out easily using water and a rag or a stiff brush.

Printing

Place the screen on the fabric with the stapled side downwards. Mix some paint in a jar according to the manufacturer's instructions and pour some of it onto the screen. Hold the squeegee firmly and, exerting pressure, draw it towards you over the screen. The squeegee will press the paint through the mesh, thus printing the image onto the fabric. Move the screen to the position required for the next pattern repeat and proceed as before. In design I the simple spot pattern is produced by using only the paper stencil. In design II, using the spot stencil affixed to the screen with dabs of filler, a square has been drawn round it on the inside of the screen and the area around the square filled in to the edge of the screen with a brush and filler (*g*).

To clean the screen

Remove any paper stencils and place the screen, stapled side downwards, on some layers of newspaper. Pour white spirit onto the inside of the screen, enough to cover it, and rub the screen hard with small pieces of cotton rag. Remove the screen from the newspaper, prop it up at one end, and clean further with fresh rag and white spirit. Finally clean the mesh with Polyclens using a small piece of rag on each side of the screen and rubbing these two pieces very firmly against one another. Make sure that no haze of ink is left in the mesh. If filler has been used, this should now be removed with water. The screen can then be used again.

Patchwork

Whole garments can be put together with patched pieces, with amusing results – either in stripes, squares, more complicated patchwork patterns or randomly, according to the nature of the design for the costume. Parti-coloured costumes are really a form of patchwork, and this is an excellent use for shorter lengths of fabric.

Another way to use patches very decoratively is to appliqué the pieces of material onto a plain base – for instance, on costumes made in a simple, cheap fabric such as unbleached calico as for the Harlequin and Columbine on page 91 (*i* and *j*). Patches can also be appliquéd on to firm net. It is not necessary to turn under the edges of the patches, they can be sewn on by machine with a zig-zag stitch. If a machine with a zig-zag is not available, cut out the patches with pinking shears to prevent fraying. A variety of different textured fabrics should be used so that the various surfaces – velvet, silk, satin or glitter fabrics – will take and reflect the light in different ways.

Quilting

A number of costumes call for fabrics that have plenty of body in them. This quality, and the way such fabrics take folds, will influence the final shape of the costume as well as the stance and movements of the wearer. It is essential for the Elizabethan period (page 98) and can be useful in peasant costumes (for example, the Afghan merchant on page 92). Genuinely heavy materials are expensive to buy, but this method of building up a fabric is simple and economical.

The best fabric base is an old blanket. Blankets come in various thicknesses and some well-worn ones can be very thin, soft and pliable. The thickness of the blanket will affect the look of the garment. Onto this backing almost any fabric, plain or patterned, can be quilted. Set out the work as shown on page 92 (a). Spread the blanket on a large table and place the surface material on top; smooth it carefully and pin it down all over. Decide on the pattern of the stitch lines – whether they are to be parallel lines, diagonals forming diamonds, lines at right angles forming squares or a decorative design more like embroidery – for example, the seventeenth-century bodice on page 92 (d). The stitching should be done with a crewel needle and embroidery cotton with the stitch illustrated (a) – a long stitch on the underside and a short stitch on top.

If the material being quilted needs to be painted in stripes or tie-dyed, this must of course be done before it is quilted to the blanket. Other decorative work is better done after the quilting process is completed. Free painting, appliqué and some kinds of printing give a more pleasing quality if done at this stage (b), and the addition of bugle beads or small mirrors will give an attractive glint under lighting.

A band of quilting round the hem of a petticoat or skirt is not only a decorative feature but will also help to give a good shape to the skirt; (e) shows a skirt of the 1850s. Moslem caps are often quilted; (f) is a child's cap from India.

Cut work

As an alternative to lace edging this method makes an attractive, crisp and theatrical finish. Use a firm fabric such as calico and draw the design on to the item of costume. Cut the open areas away carefully with sharp-pointed embroidery scissors and then machine the edges with a medium-close zig-zag stitch (page 95, d, e and f).

9 Emphasis on heads

The head is always an integral part of any costume design. However excellent the costume, if the hairstyle or headdress is wrong there will be an uncomfortable sense of wrongness about the whole appearance.

It is worth considering using the head as a very special part of the design – for example, for a stylized production in which the hat, headdress or mask is the main feature of a performer's appearance and the rest of the costume is reduced to the simplest, most basic state. This idea can also be useful if you are working to a small budget.

At some periods of history, the head is very exaggerated by the headgear: for example, the high, powdered wigs of the eighteenth century, the amazing hats of the French *Directoire*, the fantastic bonnets and hats of the eighteen-thirties and the large hairstyles and enormous hats of the Edwardians. These are worth studying. Bear in mind that a large hat will require a large wig.

It is essential to give plenty of thought to the proportion of the headdress in relation to the overall figure. Some points are vital: it must be big enough; it must be light and very securely fixed to the head; and it must also be well balanced. Actors will need ample time to rehearse in their headdresses so that they are familiar with the feel of them and can discover how close to one another they can move and stand.

There are various types of foundation on which to construct headgear. Some examples are shown with explanatory diagrams on pages 102 and 103. A firm, light-weight foundation for turbans and some hats and masks can be made by covering a balloon with papier mâché (page 102, *a*). Blow up a balloon to the size required and smear it all over with a *thin* layer of petroleum jelly. Mix some cold water paste (wallpaper paste) and tear up a large quantity of tissue paper. Cover the balloon by pasting on to it the pieces of paper until there are about six layers, then allow to dry *slowly* in a warm room; under no circumstances dry in front of a radiator or in sunshine, or the balloon will swell and burst. (Although newspaper is often recommended for papier mâché, tissue paper gives a lighter result when used on a balloon base.)

The papier mâché will take quite a time to dry, so do not be tempted to rush the process. When it is completely dry and hard, allow the air to escape slowly from the balloon – do not panic if there is some crumpling of the paper shape, it can be re-inflated by blowing gently into it. Cut off the lower part with a sharp knife so that the opening fits the head at the level required for the headdress, and strengthen the cut edge by pasting net round the area and binding it with more strips of paper. The illustration on page 103 (*b*) shows a mammoth turban from an eighteenth-century Turkish miniature built up on this type of base. To keep the turban light, use a flimsy but crisp fabric such as organdie or net for the drapery.

However large a hat is to be when finished, the inside crown must sit firmly on the wearer's head. Small rush baskets, which can be bought cheaply from charity shops, make firm crowns to which can be stitched brims cut from millinery buckram or from old straw hats (page 102, *b*). Cut a hole smaller than the circumference of the basket crown and nick it at intervals so that the tabs can be stitched in place round the edge of the crown. It is advisable to wire the brim of any hat and then to bind it or to edge it in

Constructions *for headdress*

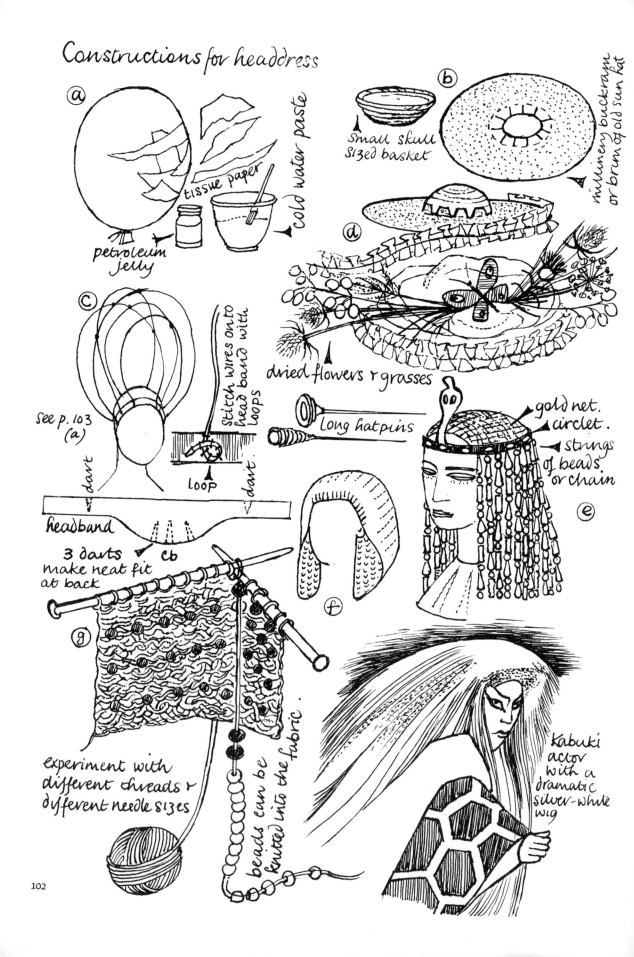

(a)
tissue paper
cold water paste
petroleum jelly

(b)
small skull sized basket
milinery buckram or brim of old sun hat

(d)
dried flowers & grasses

(c)
see p. 103 (a)
stitch wires onto head band with loops
LOOP
dart
dart
headband
3 darts make neat fit at back
cb

Long hatpins

(e)
gold net circlet.
strings of beads or chain

(f)

(g)
experiment with different threads & different needle sizes
beads can be knitted into the fabric.

Kabuki actor with a dramatic silver-white wig

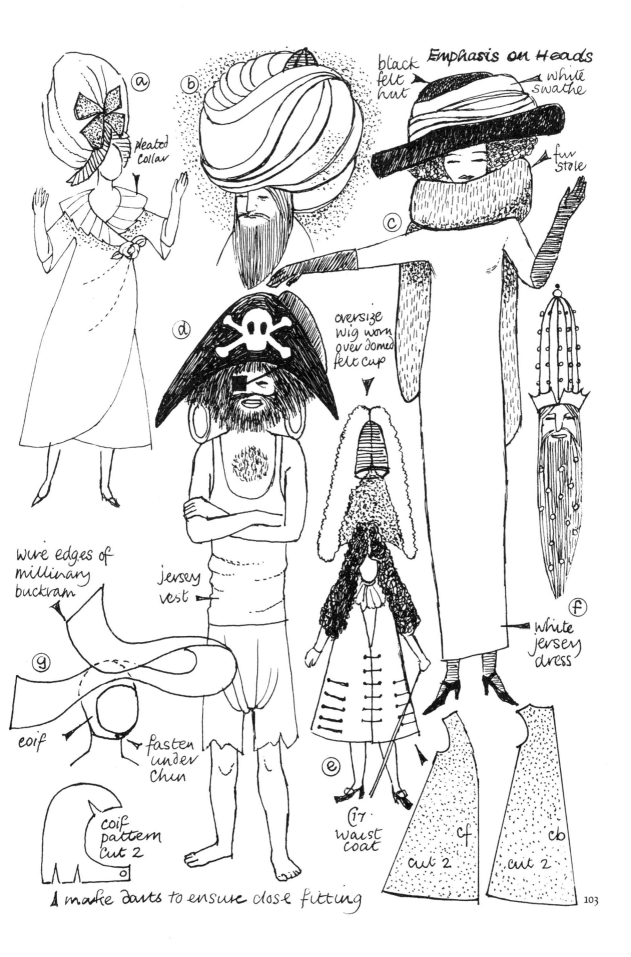

ⓐ pleated collar

ⓑ

Emphasis on Heads

black felt hat

white swathe

ⓒ fur stole

ⓓ

oversize wig worn over domed felt cup

ⓕ white jersey dress

wire edges of millinary buckram

ⓖ

coif

fasten under chin

jersey vest

ⓔ

(i) waist coat

coif pattern cut 2

cf. cut 2

cb cut 2

A make darts to ensure close fitting

some way – the drawing (d) shows a ruching of net which would look pretty on an Edwardian summer hat covered with swathes of tulle, net or some other light, crisp fabric and decorated with dried flowers and grasses and a gauze butterfly. Birds, birds' wings, feathers and flowers were all popular hat decorations in the late nineteenth century. For the stage there is no need to use the real thing; decoration can be elegantly created from paper or scraps of ribbon and fabric, together with sequins and beads, treating the trimmings always with as light a touch as possible.

The late eighteenth-century mob cap shown on page 103 (a) is built up on a wired foundation. First fit a shaped headband which will grip the head firmly and then build up a structure of millinery wire loops, binding and gluing these wherever they cross to give stability (page 102, c). Fit a cap of organdie, net or other gauzy fabric over the wire base and trim with ribbons and frilling.

A wig for an ancient Egyptian can be made from strands of beads, or beads and chain, attached to the edge of a gold net cap (page 102, e). Stitch the strands closely together to get a dense wig and finish off with a circlet placed at the point where the strands of beads are fixed to the cap. This, unlike the other examples, is a heavy headdress; the weight keeps the net cap in place on the head but allows the wearer limited movement.

Another Egyptian wig (f) can be knitted with heavy cotton or silk, as can the seventeenth-century wig on page 103 (e) which is fitted over a domed felt cap to attain the necessary height. Various threads could be used for knitting – for example, string, raffia, plastic raffia (very effective as it is crisp and shiny), or chenille (which can be unravelled from old chenille tablecloths if they can be obtained). Long strands of chenille stitched to a skull cap makes weird and mysterious hair for witches or long mermaid's tresses.

For extra texture or glitter, beads can be twisted into knitting as it progresses. Thread a quantity of beads or sequins on to a length of thread and pass the strand round the needles, spacing out the beads or sequins as the work progresses. Experiment with small pieces of knitting (page 102, g) using different stitches, sizes of needles and bead spacing. An eighteenth-century wig of white and silver thread could, for instance, be spangled with pearl beads. On page 103 (f) there is a magician's beard, made magical by threading shiny silver beads (such as can be bought in strands to decorate a Christmas tree) on to a beard built up of white and grey silk threads. The beads will need to be fixed to the threads with a tiny blob of adhesive which must be allowed to dry before these strands are added to the beard.

When building up a beard or wig, place the foundation on a wig block. Start with the lowest strands and work row by row until the uppermost row is reached. The very theatrical Kabuki wig on page 102 (h) could be built up on a felt cap using plastic raffia – splitting the raffia for the top layers to achieve a finer effect.

For a pirate (page 103, d) – perhaps for *Peter Pan* – an outsize bicorne hat over a wig of black straw could be accompanied by earrings on a similar scale. An exuberant wimple for a medieval lady or a nun (g) can be made of white millinery buckram wired round the edge and fixed to a well-fitting coif.

10 Animal and bird costumes

To be successful, animal costumes must disguise the shape of the wearer's body or the result will be a humanized animal – which is why, in most cases, the use of a tight-fitting leotard is unsatisfactory. Likewise, a very realistic animal shape is seldom entirely convincing. An adaptation or stylized costume that brings out the character and spirit of the animal rather than its anatomical characteristics must therefore be devised. The costume should allow the performer to make the necessary movements, so some observation of the real animal is helpful, and before progressing too far with the design it is important to spend some time watching the actor rehearsing. The weight and heat of the costume also needs to be borne in mind – although sometimes a degree of limitation created by the costume may help the performer to get the feel of the creature he is portraying. If tails and wings are involved, time to practise with these is essential so that they become part of the actor and not an encumbrance.

A loose, all-in-one garment can form a good basis in many instances. A pattern for this is given on page 107 and can be made with or without sleeves. It should fit easily, giving plenty of room for movement, and the cutting lines can easily be adapted to accommodate paddings worn underneath. The garment should fasten at the centre back with a long zipper. For a loose-skinned animal use a jersey fabric, but for a firmer surface unbleached calico is better.

The same pattern can be used for the owl costume, page 106 (a) or, without legs, for the eagle (c). The eagle's leggings are made from a trouser pattern, the legs cut extra long and then ruched: a length of rufflette curtain tape stitched centre front and centre back of the legs and then drawn up can be used for this. The pattern can be adapted for the Frog Prince (page 107, a): cut the leg holes large enough to accommodate padded tights. The papier mâché mask is fixed to a skull cap, with an elastic strap securing it under the chin. Further elastic straps fixed to the mask and passed under the arms will hold the headpiece firmly in place. Cut away a large mouth opening and cover this with net so that the wearer can see where he is going. Flipper feet and long canvas gloves with oversize hands complete the costume, which can then be painted or sprayed appropriately.

For the turtle (b), use a stiffened net such as marquisette nylon for the headpiece. Cut two shell shapes in flexible card for the body, and fix them loosely together with straps in the manner of a sandwich-board; this will be much quicker and easier than building up a shell shape in papier mâché, although some designers may prefer to do this. For extra durability paste a backing of scrim onto the card.

The two-man cow (c) is explained by the drawing. Easier than making a mask to fit the front man is to make a head with handles which can be used rather like manipulating a puppet. This also gives much more variety of movement.

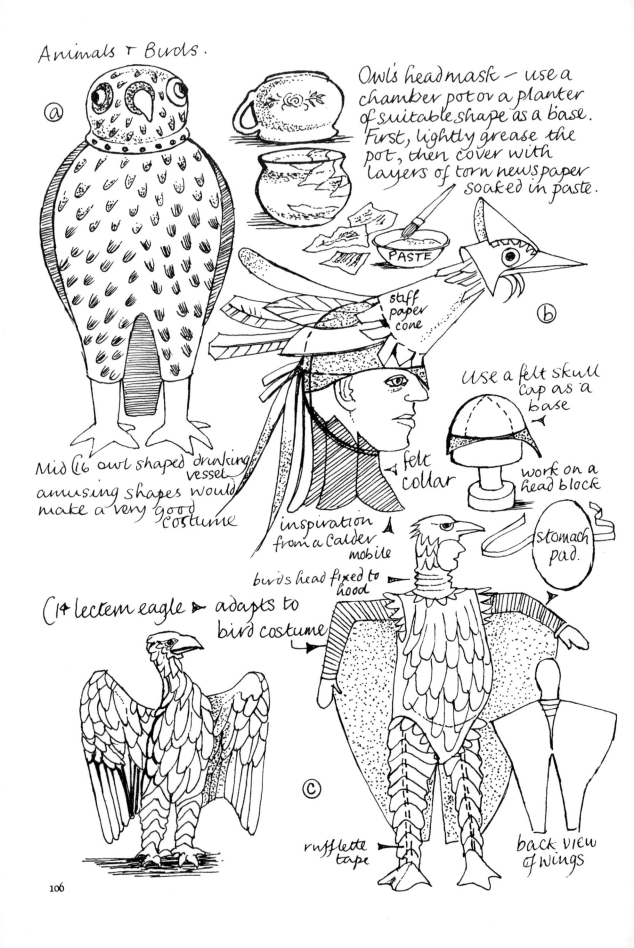

Animals + Birds.

(a)

Owl's headmask — use a chamber pot or a planter of suitable shape as a base. First, lightly grease the pot, then cover with layers of torn newspaper soaked in paste.

PASTE

stiff paper cone

(b)

Mid C16 owl shaped drinking vessel amusing shapes would make a very good costume

felt collar

Use a felt skull cap as a base

work on a head block

inspiration from a Calder mobile

bird's head fixed to hood

stomach pad.

C14 lectern eagle ▶ adapts to bird costume ◀

(c)

rufflette tape

back view of wings

Bird and Animal Costumes

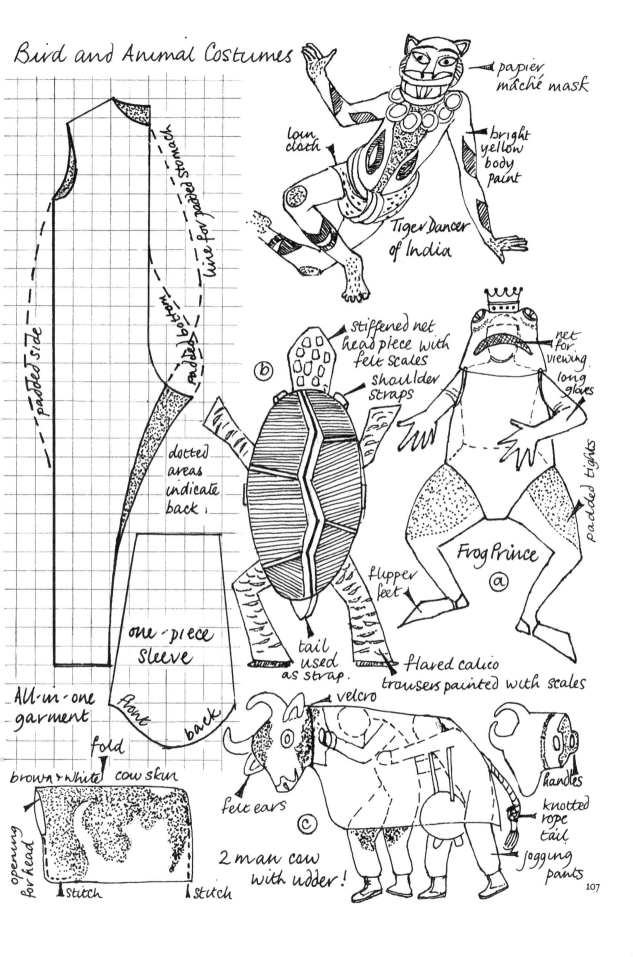

papier mâché mask

loin cloth

bright yellow body paint

Tiger Dancer of India

line for padded stomach

padded bottom

padded side

dotted areas indicate back.

one-piece sleeve

All-in-one garment

front

back

fold

brown + white   cow skin

opening for head

stitch   stitch

ⓑ

stiffened net head piece with felt scales

shoulder straps

tail used as strap.

net for viewing

long gloves

padded tights

Frog Prince

ⓐ

flipper feet

flared calico trousers painted with scales

velcro

felt ears

ⓒ

2 man cow with udder!

handles

knotted rope tail

jogging pants

11 Masks

A mask, like a headdress, may be an integral part of a costume, or it may constitute the most important part of the design with the actor wearing simply a boiler suit or some other indeterminate garment. A mask may be the element of the design that crystallizes the character; or, as in the case of the chorus in Greek drama, masks can impart anonymity and uniformity to a group of performers. Individual actors in a group may be distracting but if they are masked their corporate presence becomes of special importance.

Sometimes a very simple statement can be arresting. Among the masks shown on page 109, the coloured girl has a white mask painted on her face – a startling piece of design (c). The use of black face masks – either full or half-masks – is a feature of the Commedia dell'Arte. Two examples of masked Venetian aristocrats are shown: the seventeenth-century figure wears a simple black domino mask (d), and the figure from a Pietro Longhi painting wears a dead-white mask made dramatic by the fact that it is totally framed in black; the veil or cloak over which the black tricorne hat is worn adds to the air of mystery.

Many cultures make use of ritual masks, often involving the use of natural materials such as feathers, shells, leaves, hair and grasses. The selection of masks illustrated here gives only a small idea of the possibilities in this field – ethnic, theatrical or merely for disguise. All of the examples can be built up with papier mâché or cut out from buckram or marquisette nylon which can be stiffened with shellac.

The buffalo mask (b) can be constructed with cardboard shapes, plastic tubing and masses of garden raffia – the latter could also be used to disguise the whole body. The crow's mask (a) is fitted onto a hood with velcro, which will hold it firmly in place. The very smooth and simple design needs some textural embellishment to bring out its special quality and this can be provided by the formal arrangement of feathers, leather or fabric on the hood; a material with a sheen would be particularly appropriate to represent the appearance of a crow's plumage.

There are many elegant mask shapes with clean-cut lines in ancient Egyptian wall decoration; an example of Anubis, the jackal-headed god, is shown at the top of the page. The simple whitewashed mud sculpture of a bull or cow (f) could be adapted to create a cardboard-box mask (see chapter 14, Carnival Costumes). For the orang-utan (g), which is inspired by a screen print by Andy Warhol, use the balloon method described on page 000, adding the snout part as a separate piece, and paper strips for hair and beard. The painting should be kept very simple and unrealistic for this type of stylized mask.

Before embarking on your own designs, there are some other important sources for research. One culture which relies particularly on the mask in its traditional drama is the Japanese: in the impressive Noh drama and the puppet plays of the Bunraku, masks have become works of great refinement. Puppet theatre in many countries provides good ideas, both in the carved heads and also even the shadow figures, which have been developed to a very sophisticated degree.

Make a habit of cutting out pictures from magazines or other sources to file away as a useful and easily available background to future work.

Some Masks

(a)

Egyptian mask of Anubis

use plastic tubing

use garden raffia

horse's head (Rajasthan)

(b)

crows mask (eskimo)

balloon base

(g)

add on extra shape

Buffalo mask from Upper Volta

(f)

horned mud sculpture (construct mask from cardboard box.

hand mask

Venetian domino mask

(d)

Pietro Longhi Masked figure

(e)

(c)

Devil Dancer Sri Lanka.

109

Making papier mâché and latex masks

For a one-off job the mask can be made directly from a modelled form. If a number of identical masks is needed it is best to make a plaster mould.

First make a working drawing: take basic measurements – chin to hairline, face width, position of nose and eyes etc. – and draft them on to a modelling board (*b*). Take a lump of clay or plasticine (*a*) and model the mask on the board, remembering that the contour will need to fit the face comfortably. Finish the clay smoothly, then brush the surface with petroleum jelly, making sure that it is completely covered. Make up some cold water (wallpaper) paste, then paste about six layers of torn newspaper pieces over the clay form (*d*) and allow to dry slowly. When completely dry, ease the mask away from the clay using your fingers and a blunt knife (*c*). Paste another layer of paper onto the inside of the mask and when this is quite dry give it a coat of shellac to harden it. With a sharp blade, cut out spaces for eyes, nose and mouth that will allow the wearer to see and breathe easily.

The mask is now ready for painting. It is a good idea to give it a flat coat of a suitable colour before starting on the detailed painting. Use emulsion, acrylic or poster paint; poster paint will need varnishing when dry. Small pieces of foil or foil paper pasted on will catch the light and glint pleasingly.

To make a plaster cast, fix a cardboard wall round the clay model with gummed tape (*f*) to prevent the plaster running away. Always add the plaster of Paris to the water, not the other way round. To make sure there are no lumps, sieve the plaster into a bowl of water. Let a mound of plaster rise above the water before beginning to mix it in with the left hand while continuing to sieve with the right; this must be done quickly, as the mixture begins to stiffen in a very short time. The operation is not difficult, although it may seem tricky at first.

The plaster must be applied to the mould in two layers. For the first coat, a thin, runny mixture should be used; this is dribbled over the surface of the clay until it is completely covered, with no gaps or air bubbles left. The second layer should be thicker (*g*), using plaster of a consistency that will coat a wooden spoon thickly. Leave the cast to set. Then peel away the cardboard wall and remove the clay from the plaster cast. Wash the inside of the cast with a brush and soapy water, removing any clay particles that may be lodged in corners. When absolutely dry, grease the inside of the cast thoroughly with petroleum jelly, making sure every crevice is penetrated. Line the plaster mould with six layers of pasted torn-up newspaper (*h*) and leave until quite dry. After removing the mask from the mould, paste two layers of tissue paper onto the outer surface for a better finish. Cut holes for the eyes, nose and mouth as before and fix eyelets at the sides to take tapes or elastic.

These papier mâché masks can be adapted to make a half-mask or a stick mask.

The plaster cast can also be used as a mould for a latex mask. In this case, do NOT grease the mould, but heat it in a slow oven before filling it with latex solution (obtainable in a can). Leave in a warm place for about ten minutes – experience will teach you exactly how long – and then pour the excess latex back into the can. Leave the mould in a warm place until the latex is dry, then gently ease out the mask, trim with scissors and paint with acrylic colours.

For quick jobs, it is worth investigating the plastic and papier mâché masks sold by fancy dress and joke shops; with ingenuity it is sometimes possible to adapt these, thus by-passing some time-consuming processes.

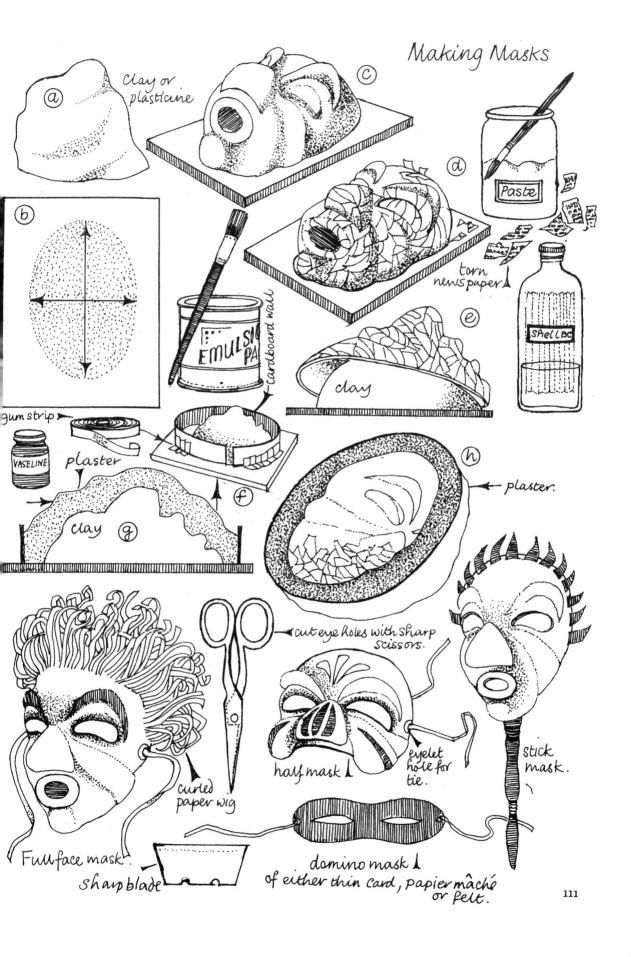

(a) Clay or plasticine

(b)

(c)

(d) Paste — torn newspaper

(e) clay

SHELLAC

EMULSION PAINT — cardboard wall

gum strip

VASELINE

plaster — clay (f) (g)

(h) plaster

cut eye holes with sharp scissors.

curled paper wig

scissors

half mask — eyelet hole for tie.

stick mask.

Full face mask.

sharp blade

domino mask
of either thin card, papier mâché
or felt.

12 Musicals, dance and opera

MUSICALS

Costumes for musicals need to have an immediate and sometimes a brash impact. They must be bold enough to register on a stage where singing, dancing and movement are vigorous and which may at times present an almost turbulent picture. When groups of performers are to be massed together, the colour co-ordination requires careful planning.

Page 113 illustrates some suggestions for very different types of musicals. The pointillist silhouette from a painting by Georges Seurat (*a*) was one of the figures used in *Sunday in the Park with George*, a production based on the painting. The design of this production was extremely sensitive, the visual images were always superb and it was an excellent example of how a painting can provide the inspiration for costume.

For *The Mikado* the cut of Japanese costume is very simple (see diagrams for happi coat and kimono) but variety and character are ensured by the fact that there are often many layers and that garments are looped into folds and tucked into an obi or, in the case of working characters, into a tie or a belt. The use of patterned fabrics gives plenty of scope for painting and printing. Kimonos are often lined in a different colour and folding back the sleeves adds contrast (*b*).

The character wearing rags and tatters (*c*) offers an opportunity to use the breaking-down techniques of patching, shredding and rough spraying, to give the appearance of a well-worn garment.

On page 119, pattern (*b*) makes an excellent fitted bodice, useful for many costumes and adaptable to a number of periods. It can be used for the girl dancer in *Oklahoma* and, teamed with a dirndl skirt, is suitable for the character of Maria in *The Sound of Music*.

DANCE

Costumes for dancers should be designed primarily for freedom of movement, which means that they must be light in weight and that the design and decoration must not impede the action in any way. Choreographers are very conscious of body line and dislike any additions to the costume which affect this. The movements demanded by the choreographer may be rhythmic, flowing, staccato, athletic, spinning, stiff and angular as in Egyptian friezes, etc. – so it is imperative to find out exactly what kind of movements the dancers will be making before embarking on the design.

The amount of fabric in a garment is important: too little will limit movement, but too much can also impede it by getting twisted round the dancer's legs, body or even neck. Although fabrics should not be heavy they must have enough weight to fall and flow well. Crepes and jerseys are good to work with and have good stretch qualities. Silks and satins will make bodices for classical ballet; these are usually cut on the lines of a Victorian bodice and, like corselets, should be lightly boned. Elasticated fabrics could be used – they hold the body firmly while allowing easy movement. Fitting sleeves into tight bodices can be a tricky procedure and it is usually necessary to insert an underarm gusset.

Avoid any sharp or pointed decorations or trimmings that could cut or scratch

Musicals

'The Mikado'

'The Mikado'
Gilbert & Sullivan

obi

b

happi coat

kimono
(back view)

c

'Sunday in the Park with George'

a

stetson
neck scarf
felt waistcoat

straw hat
pig tails
petticoat

'Oklahoma'

'Sound of Music'

russian boots

'Fiddler on the Roof'

dirndl skirt

or that might catch on to other pieces of the costume, or other dancers, causing in-extricable entanglements. Painting and appliqué are good methods for decoration. Choose buttons with care and be wary of earrings and necklaces.

Discuss and consider shoes at the outset – dancers must have comfortable shoes that are suitable and fit well, and the style of the shoe or boot and the height of the heel (if any) will influence the style of the costume. Light-coloured shoes make the feet look bigger.

Hats and headdresses must be very light and strong. Various fixings, such as elastic headbands, the use of elastic or wire loops and well-fitting skull caps, will help to keep them in place on the head. Hairpins and hatpins can be fixed into the hair or wig for extra security. Before spending too much time on the design, ask yourself how the headdress or hat is going to stay on when the dancer is moving.

If a dancer likes a costume sufficiently it is amazing how he or she will manage to work in it. Conversely, innumerable problems and snags will be discovered in a costume to which a dancer takes a dislike. Patience and tact are the designer's best stock-in-trade.

Application

Costumes for Red Riding Hood and the Wolf (page 115, *a* and *b*) are a variation from the ballet *The Sleeping Princess*, danced by the nursery-tale characters. The patterns for the girl's cloak and corselet are given on page 118; the measurements required are waist, circumference under bust, nape to skirt length, and waist to skirt length. The full skirt consists of four gores gathered into a waistband and has tucks round the hem. A simple, short-sleeved drawstring blouse is worn under the corselet.

The Wolf wears a grey-brown catsuit with dark gloves to which claws have been added (*e*) by making soft plastic or rubber finger stalls and fixing one to the end of each finger; do not use hard plastic or any sharp material that could be dangerous. Knee stockings match the gloves, or boots can be worn if suitable ones are available. For the fringes, fold a strip of fabric and cut as shown, then insert elastic in the stitched channel. For the mask (*c*), make the wolf's head in papier mâché on a base of clay (see page 106) or of crumpled chicken wire. Make a hood following the coif pattern on page 103 and place it on a head block with a skull cap on top. Stitch the cap to the hood (*d*); then place the mask on the cap and stick in place with contact adhesive. Cut fabric strips in mixed browns and greys and glue these to the mask and round the hood to make a short mane.

For the Russian peasant dancers (*g*) a dress pattern is provided on page 118. Measurements required are shoulder seam and nape to skirt length. Use a firm material such as drill which will hold a crisp shape. Either paint or appliqué the decoration, including the aprons, or use a mixture of both. The dresses are worn over white lawn or muslin blouses with drawstring necklines and puffed sleeves.

The Russian doll figure is amusing and effective, and not difficult to make, but the construction must be kept light. The size of the figure can be varied. Blow up a balloon to the required size for the head and cover with a good many layers of papier mâché strips (as described on page 101) to make a very firm shape. When dry let the air out of the balloon and, following the diagram (page 115, *h*), make slits at the base and open the tabs to make a hole into which a thin, lightweight cardboard tube can be pushed. Paste the tabs to the tube and secure it to the papier mâché head with more pasted strips – this must be a very strong join. Leave to dry, and then glue a wooden broomstick into the cardboard tube. Make the cover (see pattern on page 118) out of a lightweight fabric with three channels into which plastic or cane hoops of increasing size can be inserted. Paint or appliqué the design, including the face, and cut out a panel to be covered with

Costumes for Dance

(a)

(b)

(c)

(d)

(e)

(f)

(l)

(h)

balloon covered with papier mâché

padded arms

hoop

cardboard tube

broom stick

hoop

hoop

hoop

head square

hoop

(g)

thick dark tights or stockings

net through which the person carrying the figure can see. Stuff the arms with a lightweight filling and stitch to the top hoop so that they will swing loosely when the body is moved.

Stretch catsuits are readily available, easily fitted and allow excellent freedom of movement. They are always improved by the addition of some details or decoration, as the plain catsuit is not always very flattering to the wearer. The drawing on page 115 (i) shows a brief top made of coarse net worn over the suit. This is a very minor addition but it helps the proportion of the body. Variations are, of course, endless and can include tie-dyeing, soak-dyeing and painting.

OPERA

Operatic performances today have much more action than in the past when dramatic acting and movement were not qualities much expected of singers. Production and design are of a much higher quality than in the days when an overweight prima donna took her own costumes with her all over the world and wore them whether or not they fitted in with the general design.

Costumes for opera still need to be designed to look good on a performer who is standing still for periods of time or making only slight movements; but they must also accommodate the expansion of the rib cage as the singer breathes, and bodices should therefore be only lightly boned. Find out the kind of action and the extent of movement that is called for, and exactly what the director has in mind, before deciding on the design, and also consult the choreographer if there is one. As with costumes for ballet, the designer must become well-acquainted with the music and endeavour to express it in the lines and colour of the costumes.

Appropriate costumes can be contrived from any historical source, and the section on bold shapes (page 89) should suggest ideas suitable to many of the larger-than-life characters encountered in opera. On page 119 there is a pattern for a robe which hangs from the shoulders, gives great ease of movement and falls in graceful folds whether the singer is lying on a couch, standing, kneeling, or in fact during most of the actions he or she will be required to perform. It has the advantage of needing very little fitting, so that work can proceed when the wearer is not available. Made in a stiff fabric, it is statuesque and formal; in a soft material it will drape and flow. It can be adapted according to the design for which it is intended. It has a front opening and the centre-back seam is swung so that it can be lengthened to make a train. If it is to be worn as an over-robe the armholes should be enlarged so that the sleeves of the under-garment can slip through comfortably.

The drawings on page 117 show a few of the ways in which this robe can be painted, decorated and varied in shape. It can be very simple or very rich – or it can even be shredded into rags! The main drawing (a) is for the character Orontea in Monteverdi's *Incoronazione di Poppea*, so there are Egyptian overtones to what is basically a renaissance costume. Strands of beads are used for the wig (b) stitched to a net cap; the headdress disguises the edge of the net. Because of the weight, the wig holds its formal shape well; (it will be less heavy if plastic or papier mâché beads are used).

Three ways of adapting this pattern are shown in the drawings on page 117 (x, y and z) and explained on the pattern page. With these kinds of minor adaptations – mainly the addition of sleeves, for which two patterns are given – this robe may be used for a wide variety of characters, such as the Russian and Turkish costumes illustrated.

116

Opera.

ⓧ

bead wig

ⓐ

stencilled decoration

shoulder bosse ➤

ⓨ

front ➤

back

③

Robe with variations

Russian ➤

breast plate - use tin lids or milk bottle tops

Turk

wire

wire loops

pearl or crystal drops

ⓒ

rope

net cap

bead wig

ⓑ

ⓕ

some circlets

plastic tubing

rope

industrial felt

buckram

cord edge

ⓓ

wire struts

ⓔ

cord edging

117

Costumes for Dance

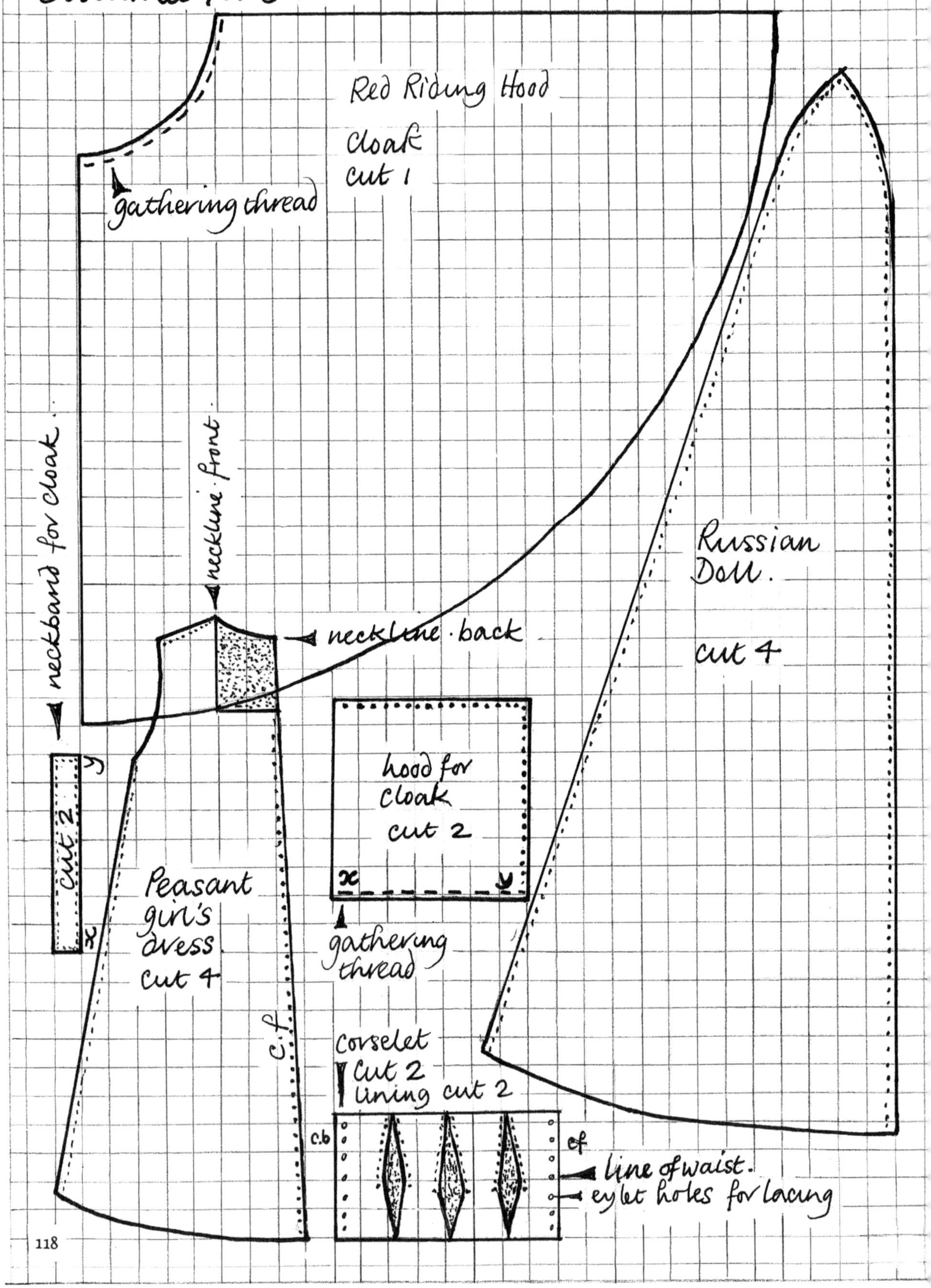

Red Riding Hood

Cloak
cut 1

gathering thread

neckband for cloak

neckline front

neckline back

Russian
Doll.

cut 4

cut 2

y

x

hood for
cloak
cut 2

Peasant
girl's
dress
cut 4

c.f.

x

gathering
thread

corselet
Cut 2
lining cut 2

c.b

c.f

line of waist.
eylet holes for lacing

Robe ⊤ Basic close fitting bodice with semi fitted sleeve.

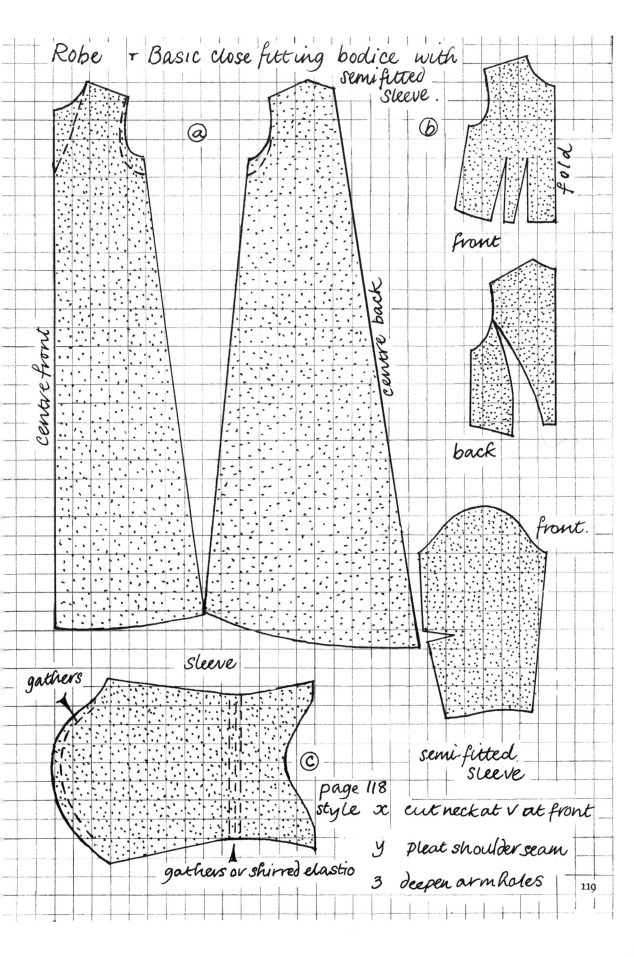

@

centre front

ⓑ

centre back

fold

front

back

front.

sleeve

gathers

ⓒ

semi-fitted sleeve

gathers or shirred elastic

page 118
style x   cut neck at v at front

y   pleat shoulder seam

3   deepen arm holes

It will often be found necessary to produce crowns as part of dance and opera costumes, and some straightforward methods are given. For dance, particularly, crowns should be very light, with tape or wire loops provided for fixing to hair or wig with hair grips. Wire bent to shape with pointed-nosed pliers and then bound with tape (c) forms the basis of a lightweight crown. After painting thoroughly with shellac it can be decorated with sequins, beads, pearls or crystal drops.

Another method is to cut the crown shape from buckram, strengthen it with millinery wire and cord the edge (e). Or the crown can be cut from industrial felt about 5mm (¼ in.) thick, using a paper pattern for the main shape, then marking out and cutting the edging shapes with a very sharp blade and gluing these in place. When the glue is dry, soak the crown thoroughly with shellac and again allow to dry before painting. Position bead knobs with long glass-headed pins, dipping each pin into a contact adhesive first to secure it.

All crowns should be thoroughly painted with shellac before any decoration is applied, as this process will produce a much stronger article.

Other drawings on page 117 show a laurel garland, a bosse trimming (f) for which barbola paste is used, and a selection of circlets. When painting costume props of any kind, first give them a coat of a suitable neutral colour using emulsion or acrylic paint. Then apply the metallic paint loosely – too dense a finish of metallic paint looks very flat and tawdry.

13 Ethnic costume

In today's multi-racial society most people have some awareness of ethnic dress and are as familiar with the appearance of a sari as they are with T-shirts and jeans. Television has also made us all more aware of very diversely dressed people, from sparsely clothed tribes in the rain forests to fur-clad Eskimos, and has demonstrated that these clothes are practical everyday wear and not some unlikely or amusing fancy dress. When assembling ethnic costumes for plays or festivals the most important qualities to aim for are naturalness, reality and authenticity. An authentic appearance can be achieved by simplification and selection and the right choice of fabric (weight and texture are important here) and by the correct proportion of any decoration.

When, on occasion, the design calls for a more stylized appearance, some adaptation and exaggeration will be appropriate, resulting in a theatrical version of national dress suitable for musicals such as *The King and* I, *The Mikado*, or pantomime characters such as Widow Twankey. In this situation, colours can be bolder and shapes more extreme. The cut of most ethnic dress is very simple, comprising squares, oblongs and triangles – which is usually the most convenient and economical way to cut the cloth. The woven width of the cloth also has a lot of bearing on shape – some native cloths are very narrow. Not all garments are made up – some are merely a piece of fabric (of specific length) wound round the body, for example the sari, the North African haik or the Buddhist monk's saffron robe. This saves sewing and makes laundry extremely easy. Many of the patterns given in chapter 7 for garments from simple shapes are based on or could be used for constructing ethnic costumes.

Only a very brief selection of ethnic dress can be given here as the field is so extensive, and garments not only vary according to country but are also frequently very regional within the country; and occupational costume is yet another aspect.

The diagram on page 122 will help to explain how to arrange a sari, but both this and the winding of turbans are always better done with practiced advice if possible. For the tunic and trousers of Rajasthani dress (*a*) exotic patterns are very typical. There are still some itinerant entertainers in India; in the drawing of father and son (*b*) the father's turban is wound from a length of twisted cloth or twisted cotton strands (*c*). The three Chinese peasant figures wear cotton garments, usually blue – from dark indigo to a faded, washed out colour, worn until very patched and threadbare. They shuffle along in black cloth slippers or straw sandals; their straw or rush hats with wide brims keep off the rain or sun, as does the universally carried umbrella. The fisherman (*d*) is wearing a buffalo-skin cloak, common to peasants in wet weather.

It is useful to look at the very similar dress of ordinary peasant women in different countries (page 123, *a*, *b* and *c*): the ankle-length skirts or dresses of rusty black cotton, well worn by work and exposure to the weather, are seen throughout Europe and the more western parts of the Middle East. Over these are worn dark aprons, plain or sometimes patterned with a small print. Even in hot weather, women remain well covered, often with several layers of garments; when creating a peasant costume, a convincingly bulky shape can be built up in this way. The head is covered with a coif or headscarf which can be tied in many different styles – sometimes it is put on wet so that it will mould to the head and can be pulled into neat and becoming folds. Footwear

Ethnic Costumes

① ②

Start on the right side, tuck in corner & wind sari round twice, tucking as you go.

pleat about half remaining length - still tucking in.

chinese fisherman

Japanese fowler

③

take the sari round the back, under the right arm & over the left shoulder. The end hangs down at the back.

sari worn over head

Indian itinerant entertainers

@

ⓒ

ⓑ

ⓓ

chinese straw hat

White cotton cap for food workers

straw hat with mesh cover

Chinese peasant.

Ethnic Costume

white hair

Moroccan water seller

Mexican Indians dressed for the enactment of their Passion Play

Nigerian girl

veiled woman Kuwait.

f

cowne shells

g

e

d

Crocheted cap.

a

b

Moslem reading the Koran.

snake boots

Cypriot

c

Portuguese

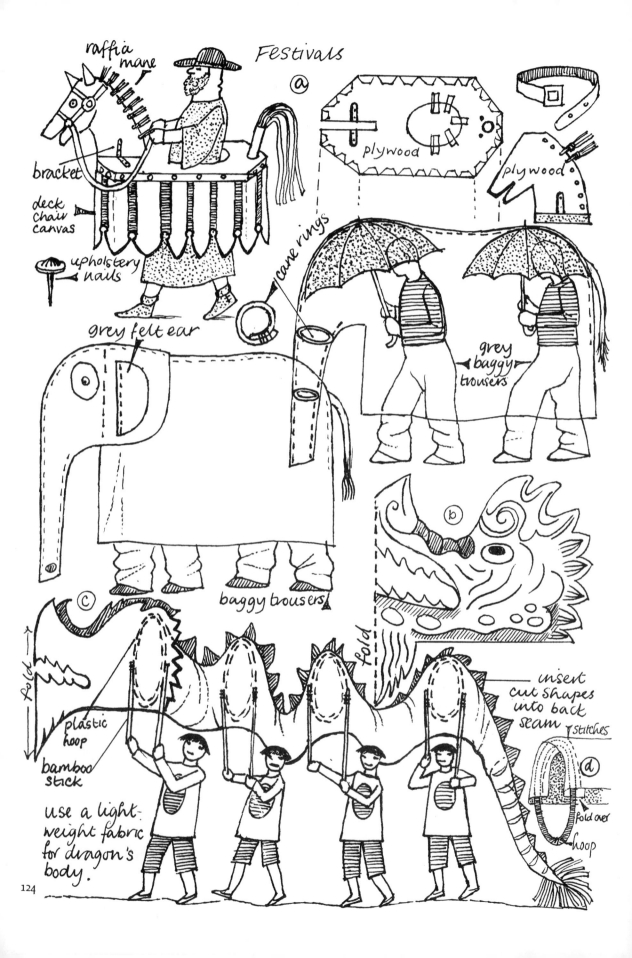

Festivals

raffia mane

@

plywood

plywood

bracket

deck chair canvas

upholstery nails

cane rings

grey felt ear

grey baggy trousers

ⓑ

baggy trousers

ⓒ

fold

fold

plastic hoop

bamboo stick

insert cut shapes into back seam

stitches

ⓓ

fold over

hoop

use a lightweight fabric for dragon's body.

varies according to the hazards under foot, and ankle bindings or boots guard against snake bites in the fields.

Many Moslem women are completely veiled (d) when they go outside their houses, although underneath their all-enveloping garment they may be wearing up-to-the-minute western dress. Faces may be covered by an embroidered mesh which allows the wearer to see where she is going, a leather face mask, or by the veil being drawn across the face and held by the teeth.

The Nigerian girl (c) is much more emancipated in her short-sleeved dress and tall turban.

The very decorative itinerant water-seller from Morocco is hung about with brass cups which he fills from a goatskin slung over his shoulder. A bell rings as he walks, advertising his presence and at the same time warding off evil spirits. His costume glitters with shiny brass discs and the hat has pom-poms and sequins dangling from the broad brim.

Three animals for use in processions

First, the hobby horse. This could feature in an English mumming play, as part of May Day merriment or to accompany Morris dancers on their peregrinations round the town. A number of them would look good in a procession of Canterbury pilgrims. For its construction, follow the diagram (a). Half-inch plywood should be cut with a fretsaw to provide body and head shapes. Glue canvas round the edge of the body, then fix loops round the hole cut out for the 'rider' to take a strong belt which will hold the horse firmly in place and leave the rider's hands free. Glue and insert the head into the slot in the body, and for extra rigidity screw brackets on each side of the neck. Paint the horse, loop raffia through holes drilled along the top edge of the neck to make a mane, and use coloured braids for the reins.

An elephant is good fun to include in Indian plays, folk tales and processions whenever there is an opportunity to do so. The ears and trunk are often painted with traditional patterns or it may wear a two-piece 'garment' decorated with patchwork designs. Here, to give the extra size and bulk necessary for an elephant, the two operators carry open umbrellas to support the body. Use an old sheet to make the pattern for the body and head coverings. To do this, fasten the open umbrellas to chairs, hat stands or some other fixture of suitable height. Drape the sheet over the umbrellas and mark and cut the shape. The finished covers should be made of a firm fabric which is soft enough to drape; if possible, back it with an old blanket to give it substance. Make rings of cane or plastic (cut from plastic bottles) to shape the trunk. Baggy, over-long grey trousers worn by the two operators will look like elephant's legs.

The Chinese New Year is a time of great celebration and the dragon shown here is not difficult to construct. It is essential that the body is made from a very lightweight fabric such as cheap nylon. Cut two long tapering shapes for the body and tail and stitch them together along the top edge, inserting triangles of paper as you go. Fix bamboo sticks to plastic or cane hoops by tying, securing the knots to the hoops with glue. Then tie the tops of the hoops inside the dragon's back with tapes and secure them at side points as well. Fold and stitch the fabric at the front end over the front hoop (d). Rings of diminishing sizes can be inserted in the tail, as with the elephant's trunk above. The dragon's head is cut from lightweight card, folded at the front (b and c), and is then glued and tied to the front hoop. Paint brightly with a fearsome design.

Not many traditional English festivals are celebrated today, but efforts to revive past customs are made from time to time in towns and villages and it may be that

Festivals.

Jack i' the Green

green sweater

b

woollen gloves – stitch twigs to fingers

green wellington boots

tissue paper

d

wire

thread pearls or beads on wires

e

top hat with ribbons

a

sash

ribbons

bells

Morris dancer
Ribbons buttons + bells

c

MAY QUEEN

Witch
semi circular tiered coat

paper doyleys

paper flowers

Welsh costume

tiny check apron

brown cotton

circular cloak

Bat

Pumpkin

trimming for May Queen's train

red & black striped skirt

⊕

button

paper petals

126

enthusiasm for them will grow. Teams of Morris dancers are increasingly active, with rallies at the Albert Hall in London and international folk-dance gatherings. The costumes worn by the dancers vary slightly from district to district, as do the dances they perform, but basically bells, ribbons and flowers are added to shirts, trousers and waistcoats (page 126, *a*). Straw hats or top hats are embellished in the same way, and the dancers carry handkerchiefs or short staves. Originally all the dancers were men; girls who now find a place in the team wear full, decorated skirts.

Jack-i'-the-Green is a character of doubtful origin but he appears in several English country festivals, clad from head to foot in leaves (*b*). It is best, if possible, to use evergreens, which will last longer, and to stitch them on to a sacking shape; (one source recounts the use of a pyramid shape – 'a walking pyramid of leaves and flowers'). He makes an appearance on May Day, and has been known to take part in midsummer celebrations, with mummers at Christmas, and in first-footing at New Year. In the drawing he wears an old top hat sprouting with leaves and a long green beard. The sign-boards of pubs called The Green Man often depict this character.

The crowning of the May Queen (*c*), with a background of maypole dancing, was once a feature of English May Day festivities – it can still be found as a survival or revival on some village greens. The participants, children or young people, traditionally wore white – dresses for girls, shirts and trousers for boys, perhaps with added sashes. Real flowers were picked from the hedgerows for decoration, an activity which would be frowned on today when the conservation of wild flowers is all-important – but tissue paper flowers are very pretty and easy to make as an alternative (*d*). Cut petal-shaped discs in two or three sizes, and some fringed stamens. Thread the stamens through a wire looped at the end, dab contact adhesive in the centres of the petals, thread these on to the wire and pinch them together, pleating the tissue discs into a flower-like shape. These flowers can be wired on to the circlet at the base of the crown. Wires attached to the circlet have beads threaded on to them before being bent together in the centre (*e*) where they are wired together and secured with a blob of adhesive, finished with a larger bead. Paper flowers for the dress can be made without the wire and stitched into position. (They can also be threaded on to strings to make garlands, or wired into a bouquet.) The May Queen's net train is edged with daisies.

Hallowe'en is still celebrated with parties, pumpkin lanterns and revellers dressed as creatures of darkness, ghosts, witches, warlocks, worricows and many more. Try to avoid the commonplace and to bring some design into the characters being represented. A cloak stuck with silver paper stars is not good enough! The witch's cloak (page 126, *f*) is inspired by a highwayman's cloak with tiered capes, the edges being cut into points. Round her neck is a black net ruffle. Underneath the cloak, a black jumper is worn over a skirt of red and black stripes – or it could be diamonds or patchwork. Black stockings and shoes to which extra points have been glued complete the costume. Other creatures can be devised – the bat on page 126 wears a circular painted cloak. *The Garden of Delights*, a painting by Hieronymus Bosch, will furnish endless ideas.

The tradition of acting bible stories has continued for many centuries in England in the form of miracle and mystery plays, of which the Chester, York and Wakefield cycles are best known and are still performed in churches or in the open air. The nativity play remains an important part of the Christmas festival, performed by schools, students and church groups and often involving choirs and musicians. On page 123 the two masked figures (*f* and *g*) are Mexican Indians, wearing the kind of clothes common to peasant workers in the region – jeans and a mixture of jackets, waistcoats and shirts put together for daily use and not for appearance. In obedience to a vow, this particular tribe dance

Festivals -
A Nativity

(a)

▶ fillet.

Joseph.

Mary

▶ simple head cloth

thick knitted 'boots' tied with cords ▶

(b)

The angel

hooded cloak

(d)

Turban with liripipe ▶

padded coat ▶

Sleeveless cotehardie ▶

(c)

(e)

(f)

2 shepherds

2 Kings or wise men.

128

the part of the Judases who torment Jesus at the enactment of the crucifixion. The wooden swords represent the weapons of Roman soldiers and the doll on a stick symbolizes a child killed by Christ's enemies. The startling masks are roughly made but very dramatic: one has silky white hair, the other's is sparser and black; the ears on both characters are important, the painting is bold and uncomplicated. The masks are probably built on boxes. Both men have anklets of cowrie shells. It would be interesting to apply this simplicity of idiom to other Christian stories such as a nativity play, using everyday clothes with masks or other symbols to identify the characters.

More traditionally, costumes for nativity plays may be based on the indigenous dress of Middle Eastern countries or, as on page 128, inspired by manuscript paintings from the medieval period. Refer to the section on medieval costume in chapter 3 of this book for more information.

14 Carnival costumes

Street carnivals and similar ephemeral events call for costumes made quickly from cheap or free materials. The design needs to be witty, lively and larger than life. Here is a chance to be gaudy and ridiculous; think how boring carefully constructed, historically correct, tasteful costumes would look processing down a noisy street! Concentrate on bulk, movement – provided, for example, by streamers and feathers – and sound, such as bells and rattles, all of which will build up to a really exaggerated result. Coloured paper, newspaper, cardboard boxes and cheap fabrics should be the basic materials. As far as possible, use a stapling machine (one with a long arm will be helpful) or a staple gun to cut down on sewing and gluing, although strong adhesives and parcel tape will also be needed, plus lots of paint and big brushes. Be sure the costume is strong enough to last the day and will not disintegrate en route; and also that the wearer can see and breathe and will not be crippled by his or her footwear before the day is over. It is really not possible to produce a rain-proof costume.

The ideas on page 131 are intended only as suggestions to trigger off even greater flights of fancy. This is an opportunity to let your imagination soar.

A *carnival grotesque* (*a*). For the body garment use the square pattern (page 85, *a*) to make a tunic instead of a coat and leave considerably deeper armholes. For the trousers, follow pattern (*e*) on the same page. Alternatively, make a very baggy all-in-one garment using the pattern on page 107. The head is made from a large cardboard box. Make a neck-sized hole in the base and two slits (*b*) so that there is room for the head to go through the neck hole. The hole for the mouth should be located so that the wearer can see through it. The hat is made from cardboard and glued to the top of the box; hang bells around the brim. The nose is a section cut from a papier mâché egg box. Spectacles are painted onto the face and the beard is thickly fringed newspaper.

Clown (*c*) For the basis of this costume use either a leotard and tights or a jumpsuit, painted or sprayed with red and blue stripes. Make a belt of double fabric with a channel through the middle. A white card cone, like a dunce's cap, is the foundation of the headdress. To form the fans, take four sheets of strong white paper 400mm (16 ins) square, paint with red and blue stripes on both sides, and fold them crisply in concertina pleats 25mm (1 in.) wide. Then fold across on a centre line and fix with adhesive. Attach two fans to the cap, as in the drawing, and the other two to the costume from waist to thigh using velcro. To keep these fans spread out, take a length of plastic whalebone, fix it along the top of one fan, slide it through the channel of the belt at the back and then fix it to the upper edge of the fan on the other side. Make a pleated ruff from paper or a crisp fabric, and decorate the arms with white bangles.

Giant Sun (*d*) Cover a child's hoop with strong paper, and cut a hole for the mouth through which the bearer can see. Paint the sun's face, giving it plenty of shine and gilding. Glue short strips of glittering paper radiating outwards round the edge. Held aloft, the face can be moved and twisted to and fro very effectively – a procession of suns could be most exciting. A simple tunic is all that is required for the bearer's costume.

Carnival Time

ⓐ

bells

reflective paper

gardening or household gloves

200 m.m.

8"

fold line

thin cardboard cone.

ⓒ

velcro

ⓔ

newspaper roll

ⓕ

maraca using yoghourt pots

ⓖ

Paper covered hoop

slits for head opening

beard line

box base

ⓑ

cover a hoop with strong paper.

ⓓ

fringed newspaper for beard

Street Carnival

newspaper hats

wool ov. string loops

elastic head band

elastic.

unravel ends.

@

TIMES

THE BAND
White sloppy cotton Tshirts
painted with narrow stripes

tape

cotton tape fringe.

with streamers attached
Unbleached calico
trousers
waist sashes
joke shop hat.

streamers

cut buttons from plastic containers

b

bowler hat with ribbons

magnets

Bear's head papier mâché & cardboard.

bear's skin made from brown sacks

d

HURDY GURDY MAN
old over-large frock coat —
waistcoat from flags

Trousers — painted checks trimmed with pattern of plastic buttons

zipped slipper boot

Sacks stitched all over with rags

c

carpet slippers

132

Paper favours (page 131, *e*) can be quickly made. Roll some newspaper and secure it temporarily with two elastic bands. Dip one end in brilliantly coloured dye or paint and, when it is dry, shred it with a sharp knife. Remove the bands and, holding the lower part, slightly ease the roll and push the centre upwards for several centimetres. Secure it tightly with two bands of gumstrip or sellotape.

Maraca rattle (*f*) Take two yoghourt pots, preferably the large size, and make a hole large enough to take a screw in the bottom of one of them. (The best way to do this is to heat a metal point in a flame and push it, when red hot, into the plastic, revolving it until the hole is the right size.) Referring to diagram (*g*) insert the screw through a washer, the pot, and then another washer, and screw it into the top of a stick. Put some beans or beads into the pot and with contact adhesive seal the edges of the two pots together.

Favours of all kinds are part of the carnival scene – streamers, ribbons, balloons on sticks will all contribute to the general appearance and mood.

Further quick and easy costumes on page 132 use very basic items and can be put together at minimum cost:

Paint sloppy T-shirts with stripes for the bandsmen (*a*); this is an easy way to achieve uniformity for a group.

Use an old flag to make a waistcoat (*b*). The hurdy-gurdy (*d*) is an easy prop to make from a cardboard box and a tape recorder can be concealed inside it.

Tear up gaudy rags and stitch or thread them into a tunic made from sacks, to be worn over a ragged sweater (*c*). Tie bells to the carpet slippers.

Brown sacking also makes the bear's skin (using the all-in-one pattern on page 107). Fix magnets to the mask and the ball.

15 Mainly for schools

For work in schools, especially with primary age groups, fairly instant costumes are the most successful because children can see and achieve results quickly. There is not usually much time available for very complicated work – nor, in most cases, is this suitable. It is also desirable that the children take an active part in making the costumes, which should therefore mostly be easy to put together with adhesives and very basic sewing.

Try to assemble a variety of garments in a dressing-up trunk. Many amusing costumes can be put together from odds and ends, and a big box of offcuts of paper, card and fabrics, wools, braids, old nylon tights etc. will be very useful; and, depending on the production in hand, an appeal for cardboard boxes, pieces of polystyrene and plastic containers will produce a good nucleus to work from. Children will find collecting things part of the fun.

Paper sacks and large strong paper bags are a great standby in the classroom; sometimes these can be obtained second-hand and if they are in good condition they will be most useful – if not, it is worth investing in a quantity from a supplier.

Scissors, good strong needles to take wool or thread, strong adhesives, staples and staple gun (in the hands of an adult), big brushes and plenty of poster paint will be all that is necessary for most basic procedures. Children will enjoy printing their own patterns on items of costume; potato printing will be suitable for young children and lino cuts for the older ones. Ensure that there is plenty of newspaper on which to spread work out and for cleaning up, as well as an endless supply of rags.

The ideas on page 135 for using paper sacks show characters for a simple play or mime based on *Punch and Judy*. The sacks can be painted or decorated with cut paper shapes pasted on to them – better still, combine the two methods, as this gives a mixture of textures, and include some foil pieces which will catch and reflect the light. Use paper rosettes (*a*) for decoration – these can be threaded on to elastic for use on shoes and Wellington boots. Diagrams show how to cut and attach Punch's traditional hump (*b*). Use an inexpensive fabric such as butter muslin to make the ruffs and mob cap. Mittens made of wool or from brightly coloured felt will give the hands a puppet look and T-shirts and tights complete the outfits. The crocodile's tail, like Mr Punch's hump, is made from very strong paper or thin card. If the costumes are needed for several performances, the paper or card can have a thin muslin backing pasted on to it for added durability. Use a cardboard box for the basis of the crocodile's head and add cardboard jaws (*c*).

For a black and white skeleton (*e*), a tabard of thin card or felt can be fitted over a contrasting long-sleeved black or white T-shirt and trousers. The webbing straps can be fastened with stick-and-stitch velcro. Cut away the design of the ribcage from the front of the tabard. Paint the bones of the arms and legs on the sleeves of the T-shirt and the trouser legs – black on white or vice versa. Thread rug wool into woollen mittens for the hands and paint a skull onto a paper bag mask.

The robin (*d*), or any other simple bird costume, is based on brown tights and a suitably-coloured jumper. Take a small cushion, shake the filling to one end and stitch or tie the two top corners together. Attach straps as in the diagram and tie on the padding under the jumper. A knitted or crocheted shawl is ideal for the wings, but if this is not

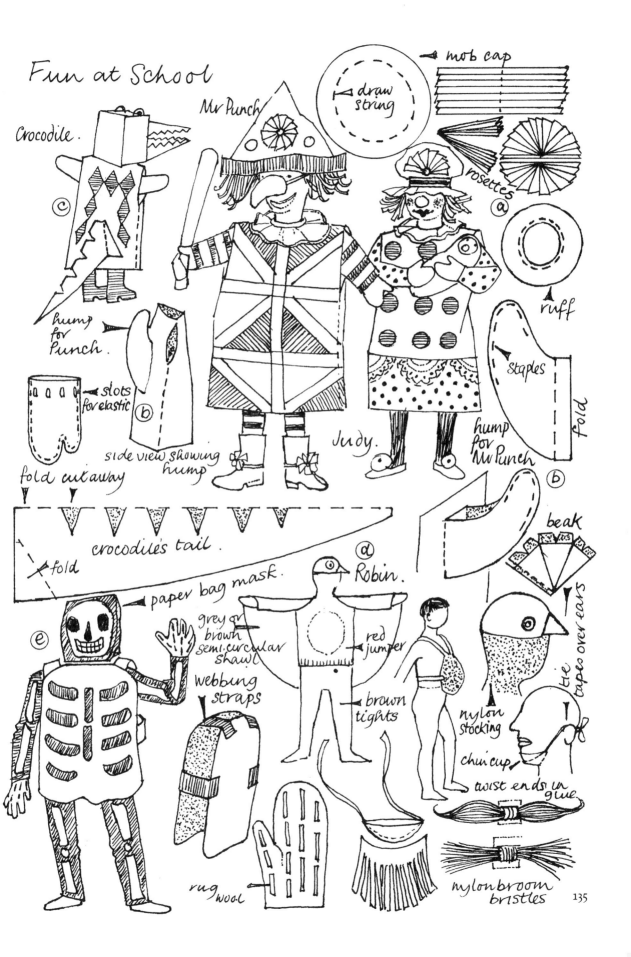

Fun at School

Crocodile.

Mr Punch

mob cap

draw string

rosettes

Crocodile ©

hump for Punch.

slots for elastic

ⓑ

fold cutaway

fold

side view showing hump

crocodile's tail.

ruff

staples

fold

hump for Mr Punch

Judy.

ⓑ

beak

paper bag mask.

ⓐ Robin.

ⓔ

grey or brown semi-circular shawl

webbing straps

red jumper

brown tights

tie tapes over ears

nylon stocking

chin cup

twist ends in glue

rug wool

nylon broom bristles

Fun at School.

(a)

cauliflower hat

(b)

(c)

SALE SALE SALE

The Sweep

Billboard man

Baker's boy

The Butcher

Milkman

(d)

Mrs Block the butcher's wife.

bosom padding

small pillow

top

chef's hat

side

paper hat

bonnet

shawl

print skirt.

washerwoman

(e)

top

Side

Top hat

brim

money bag with 3 pockets

carpenter

paper collars

Street hat seller

This style 10b

(f)

hatter

136

available a half-circular fabric cloak can be used instead. The basis of the head is a small straw basket from a charity shop with beak and eyes added. Disguise the face by pulling the foot of a nylon stocking or pair of tights over the head – it is possible to see and breathe through this and face paint can be applied to it to match it to the head.

Some suggestions for a beard and moustaches are shown (e): paper, felt, wool, stranded silks can all be used to make up different versions.

The costumes on page 136 are mainly contrived from simple items added to the child's own jeans, T-shirt, shoes etc. Dressing up is not only for plays but can be used in the classroom to extend projects and give more fun and reality to schemes in which the class is involved. The costumes shown here of workers and shopkeepers could be used for a theme such as 'Our high street in Grandfather's time'. A project like this encourages simple research into the clothes people were wearing and the reason why their clothes suited the jobs they were doing – many more characters could be added, or a country scene could be developed with farmers, shepherds and milkmaids in the cast.

The Sweep (a) wears an oversize adult shirt and patched trousers (jeans will do). Use black nylon stockings to make a sooty face mask and to cover the hands and arms. The Chef or Baker (b) needs a big apron and white cotton chef's hat (see diagram lower down the page); the trousers can be made from check dusters sewn together. Both Butcher (c) and Milkman (d) have striped aprons, and thickly ribbed socks can be used to resemble the Milkman's gaiters. The drawing for the Butcher's Wife comes from the original design for the card-game of 'Happy Families' – these cards are well worth looking at and could inspire an excellent and amusing set of costumes. The Fishmonger (not shown) would wear an apron with vertical stripes. The Carpenter (who always wears a paper cap) and the Hatter (e and f) are taken from the Tenniel illustrations for Lewis Carroll's Alice books. Street sellers of hats or old clothes sometimes wore a number of hats piled on top of one another and amusing touches like this give life to a production.

Two diagrams are given for paper collars: cut from thin card and notched along the folded edge, they will give a period look to the characters. Fasten them in front with a small piece of double-sided adhesive tape.

When building up costumes such as these, consider the proportion of each element and be sure to make good use of colour so that the final result is lively, even at the risk of losing realism.

16 Costumes for video

Now that the video camera has become accessible to so many people and is used as an adjunct to many projects and activities in schools and colleges, it may be useful to consider the best way to design costumes for filming. In productions for the theatre, the complete costume is always visible and the action takes place within a defined area – the stage set. Although the eye of the audience may be focussed on a single character or set of characters, it is always looking at entire figures. Not so with video: the video camera, like the film or television camera, has a selective eye. The selection is made by the director and the camera man, who choose how much or how little of the scene before them they will show. In long shots, figures become very small so that very little of what an actor is wearing registers; but as the camera moves in, more and more detail emerges and is of tremendous importance. This means that much more attention must be given to the minutiae of costume, the use of small details expressing character, and the quality of finish.

In the theatre a well-worn costume for a rough character can – and should – be broken down broadly, patched, ripped and splashed with paint. Such bold treatment would appear ridiculously exaggerated on camera. Breaking down becomes a very subtle art – rough dyeing, followed by the use of a cake of soap applied to the edges of cuffs and collars to suggest stains and dirt, fraying with sandpaper and cheese grater, and finally the judicious use of a spray gun, is the procedure to be followed.

Variety of texture takes on much greater importance and should be fully exploited. Often it is more important than pattern, which must be used with discretion if it is not to be a distraction. Care is needed with colour too; quite small items such as handbags can very easily be a distraction on camera. Shoes, gloves, and ties are another area where jarring colour or detail can be particularly irritating – television newscasters' and commentators' ties are a case in point.

Beware of over-large patterns which may distort shape, unless they are to be used for a particular purpose, or of very small ones which can be too busy. Also take care that (except for a specific reason) actors wearing loudly checked or striped suits or actresses in patterned dresses do not disappear into patterned chairs or settees on which they may be directed to sit. Necklines take on a great deal of importance, because in close shot necks may be cut off awkwardly – a low neckline might create the impression that the character was naked. Outfits should not be so asymmetric that they appear like two different garments in cross-cutting shots. Brims on hats must be watched in case they cast too much shadow and hide important facial expression, although in the right situation a heavy shadow can provide mystery.

A word of warning regarding continuity – be sure to have a well-marked script with all costume details accurately and fully annotated for each scene so that there will be no shaming calamities when scenes are shot out of sequence.

A last word: if a costume is going to be damaged during the action, or if the actor is going to be thrown into a lake, be sure there are duplicate costumes in readiness.

Finale

For a production that is to run for several performances it is important that energy and enthusiasm should not flag before the first night arrives, but it is equally important that planning and organization should not deteriorate as excitement and exhaustion increase. Check that all adjustments decided on at dress rehearsals have been carried out and that all additions and details have been accounted for and last-minute purchases made. Assemble each artist's costumes and props and check them carefully against the costume lists so that there is no need for a frantic search for shoes, gloves or other easily mislaid items just before the curtain goes up. See that everything is freshly pressed, and in the excitement of the moment do not forget to monitor the heat of the iron and do not hang costumes close to dressing room lights, which become very hot. Have safety pins, needles and thread to hand and spare zippers of different length available for quick replacement if necessary.

Prevent actors from eating and drinking once they are wearing their costumes – many disasters have occurred in this way – and from creasing their freshly prepared garments by sitting carelessly. Above all, behave with calmness and confidence during the mounting tension. Despite the excitement, at the end of the performance collect and check methodically all costumes, particularly small items. List and put aside all articles that need to be laundered, and list any repairs that need doing. Complete this before going to any first-night celebrations or the next day will be full of problems.

Before the second performance, find out from the wardrobe team whether there have been any problems and see that these are sorted out, and assure yourself that arrangements for cleaning, pressing etc. are working smoothly and that the costumes will be fresh, ready and properly checked. Ensure that they are in the dressing rooms in good time.

At the end of the run, take a long, cool look and decide where and how there could have been improvements and in what way these could be implemented next time. Sort the costumes, deciding which ones to hold for stock and which are expendable. Salvage buttons and trimmings and store these in labelled boxes and plastic bags. Everything should be washed and cleaned before it is put away.

All will now be ready for the next time – and with added knowledge and experience each production should be an improvement on the one before.

Some words about materials

The availability of fabrics and haberdashery, which are part of the costume designer's and costume maker's stock-in-trade, is constantly changing. Excellent new materials come into the shops, but equally excellent ones disappear or are replaced by less useful versions. Fabric departments in large stores seem to be shrinking in size as home dressmaking becomes less popular. The following goods are still to be found in a good department store and, if there are sufficient funds, it is as well to fill the wardrobe cupboard before it is too late.

Calico bleached and unbleached.

Linen duck This has good 'body' for firm garments.

Sheeting both plain and printed; makes up well.

Organdie For collars, ruffs and ruffles, artificial flower trimmings.

Victoria lawn A fine-textured cotton, useful for wimples, coifs and shirts.

Butter muslin, mull Open-textured soft cotton for shifts and some shirts, but will not take a lot of wear.

Tarlaton, marquisette nylon (black and white), stiffened muslin These are all sold as stiffeners but can be used for ruffs, bonnets and headdresses.

Buckram For the stiffest work; can be used for crowns and headdresses.

Canvas and hair canvas These are also stiffeners but are texturally interesting and can be used for rough aprons, waistcoats etc. They are very scratchy to wear.

Felt is a very useful fabric and comes in many colours and several weights, but being made of wool it is too expensive to use freely. Small squares available from craft suppliers are useful for appliqué decoration.

Scrim Open-textured natural hemp-type cloth. Good texture for rough shirts, blouses etc.

Various iron-on stiffeners including iron-on shirt-collar canvas. (Watch the heat of the iron for these, and avoid accidentally putting the iron on the treated side of the fabric.)

Nylon horsehair braid Not many widths are available at present, but it can be machined together. Useful for some hats and trimmings.

Velcro Available in both stitch-on and stick-on varieties; very useful for masks, costume props, trick costumes. Not good for garment fastenings as it buckles and is clumsy.

Button moulds For covered buttons, available in a range of sizes.

Dylon dyes Available for hot and cold hand dyeing and machine dyeing.

Shoe paint A great help for changing the colour of shoes easily.

Shoe dye For suede shoes. Can be used on masks and costume props.

Buttons On the whole these are very poor quality today. Search for old ones.

Beads and sequins Stores have excellent selections but they can be expensive.

Boning Whalebone has been replaced by synthetic materials such as Rigilene and Poly-boning. End caps are available, a great advantage.

Padding materials:

Foam rubber can be bought in a variety of thicknesses.

Kapok is made from cotton waste and is heavy.

Synthetic-fibre wadding is light and has the advantage of being washable.

For specialist requirements, refer to Yellow Pages.

Finding out

Good reference sources are essential, and when you are working on a production there is often not much time for research, so try to acquire the habit of making notes at all times and of keeping a good filing system. At the very least it is worth keeping a note of the whereabouts of good source material.

Many museums, in addition to those that specialize in costume, have a costume department and display period garments. In most large public art galleries there will be paintings that depict costume over a large time range and often in great detail. Many museums have ethnography departments displaying masks, fabrics, decorative patterns etc. Museums and galleries usually sell postcards and useful booklets which can be kept for reference. To discover where to find the kind of material you are interested in, or what is available in your district, enlist the help of the reference department of your local library. Don't forget, too, to take a sketchbook and a camera with you when travelling, to record ideas that may inspire you later.

Books specializing in costume and fashion from a historical angle, with some cutting information, are the bones of the subject (see Bibliography); but contemporary photographs and engravings, and contemporary periodicals, particularly *Punch*, will provide a mass of information on everyday dress at all social levels; and *The National Geographic Magazine* is an excellent pictorial source for ethnic material.

Most good libraries should be able to tell you where to locate out-of-date periodicals, but before troubling them be quite clear about the dates and angle of your research.

Bibliography

BARTON, Lucy *Historic Costume for the Stage*. Black, London and Baker, Boston 1961

BOTT, Alan *Our Fathers (1870–1900)*. Heinemann, London and Arno, New York 1975

BOTT, Alan and CLEPHANE, Iris *Our Mothers*. Gollancz, London and Arno, New York 1975

BOUCHER, Francois *20,000 Years of Fashion*. Abrams, New York 1966

CONTINI, Mila *Fashion from Ancient Egypt to the Present Day*. Cresent, New York 1966

CUNNINGTON, C. Willett and Phillis *Handbooks of English Costume* (several vols covering different periods). Faber, London and Plays, Boston

CUNNINGTON, Phillis and LUCAS, Catherine *Occupational Costume in England*. Black, London and Barnes & Noble, New York 1967

DAVENPORT, Millia *The Book of Costume*. Crown, New York 1964

DE LA HAYE, A. *Fashion Sourcebook*. Macdonald Orbis, London 1988

HARTLEY, Dorothy and ELLIOT, Margaret *Life and Work of the People of England*. (6 vols) Batsford, London c.1928

HOWELL, Georgina In Vogue: Six Decades of Fashion. Allen Lane, London and Schocken, New York 1976

KOHLER, Carl and VON SICHART, Emma (ed. Alexander K. Dallas) A History of Costume. Dover, New York and London

LAVER, James A Concise History of Costume. Thames & Hudson, London 1969

LAVER, James A Concise History of Costume and Fashion. Scribner, New York 1974

LAVER, James Costume Illustration: The Seventeenth and Eighteenth Centuries. Costume Illustration: The Nineteenth Century. H.M. Stationery Office, London

NUNN, Joan Fashion in Costume 1200–1980, Herbert Press, London 1984; New Amsterdam, New York 1990

PAYNE, Blanche History of Costume from the Ancient Egyptians to the Twentieth Century. Harper & Row, New York and London 1965

PRIESTLEY, J. B. The Edwardians. Sphere Books, London 1972 and Harper & Row, New York 1970

RUPPERT, Le Costume I-V. Flammarion, Paris

SCHOEFFLER, O. E. and GALE, William Esquire's Encyclopedia of Twentieth Century Men's Fashions. McGraw-Hill, New York 1973

SCHÖNEWOLF, Herta Play with Light and Shadow. Studio Vista, London and Reinhold, New York 1969

SCHROEDER, Joseph J. (Jr) (ed.) The Wonderful World of Ladies Fashion 1850–1920. Digest Books, Northfield, Illinois 1971

TAYLOR, Boswell (ed.) Picture Reference Books nos 1, 2, 4, 5, 10 (particularly 4, Costume). Brockhampton Press, Leicester, England

TILKE, M. Costumes Patterns and Designs. Zwemmer, London 1956 and Hastings, New York 1974

WAUGH, Norah Corsets and Crinolines. Batsford, London 1987

WAUGH, Norah The Cut of Men's Clothes, 1600–1900. Faber, London and Theatre Arts, New York 1964

WAUGH, Norah The Cut of Women's Clothes, 1600–1930. Faber, London and Theatre Arts, New York 1968

WILCOX, R. Turner The Dictionary of Costume. Scribner, New York 1969 and Batsford, London 1971

WILCOX, R. Turner Five Centuries of American Costume. Scribner, New York 1963, 1976 and Black, London 1966

WINTER, Gordon A Country Camera 1844–1914. David & Charles, Newton Abbot 1971; Penguin, London 1973 and Gale, Detroit 1971; Penguin, New York 1974

Any volumes of Punch, Harper's and Vogue

Index to Text